Period Lighting

Period Lighting

Stanley Wells

PELHAM BOOKS

First published in Great Britain by Pelham Books Ltd
52 Bedford Square, London, W.C.1
1975

ISBN – 0 7207 0746 3

Printed by Hollen Street Press, Slough,
bound by Dorstel Press, Harlow

To Our Daughter
Lisette

$\mathcal{C}$ontents

Acknowledgements 10
Introduction 15

Chapter One   Italy 19
Chapter Two   France 34
Chapter Three Spain 66
Chapter Four   England 78
Chapter Five   America 130

Appendix One and Appendix Two
see List of Illustrations

Index 165

Illustrations

PLATES

1	Roman hand lamp	19
2	Hanging lamp from Pompeii	20
3	Iron Gothic lantern	23
4	*Braccio cresset*	24
5	*Torciere di ferro*	25
6	Renaissance *candelabro*	26
7	Cherub with cornucopia	27
8	*Lampada.* Sanctuary lamp	28
9	*Lampione* in French style	29
10	*Lumière* with flowers	30
11	*Candeliere Veneziano*	31
12	*Lucerna*	32
13	*Couronne de lumière pédiculées*	37
14	Renaissance *chandelier*	38
15	*Bras de lumière*	39
16	Mazarin chandelier	41
17	*Régence appliqué*	45
18	Rococo candlestick	46
19	Rococo *appliqué*	46
20	*Candle lit funeral of King Philip V*	47
21	*Lustre à cristaux*	48
22	Glass peg lamp. Eighteenth Century	51
23	Ribbon-bow *applique* c.1755	53
24	Piping boy *applique* Eighteenth Century	54
25	*Directoire applique* 1796/99	57
26	Clock and candelabrum. Late Eighteenth Century	58
27	Empire *lustre* c.1804	59
28	Empire *lustre* c.1809	60
29	Empire 'balloon'	62
30	*Lampadaire*	63
31	Student lamp	64
32	*Farol* lantern	70
33	*Final* lantern	71
34	Dragon bracket	72
35	*Corona de luz*	73
36	*Barroco* lantern case	73
37	*Lampara cornoa*	74
38	Empire bracket	75
39	Mosque lamp	77
40	Stone lamp	78
41	The Gloucester Candlestick	80
42	Tudor chandelier	83
43	Renaissance sconce	83
44	Crusader chandelier	85
45	Netherlands chandelier	86
46	Silver sconce with cherubs	89

47	Haddon Hall chandelier	90
48	Knole House chandelier	91
49	Mazarin chandelier	91
50	Silver sconce	93
51	Silver chandelier	95
52	Chandelier for the Czar	97
53	Rococo candlestick	98
54	Adam candlestick	100
55	Crystal *girandole*	101
56	Crystal chandelier	102
57	Regency 'balloon'	106
58	Wroxton Abbey chandelier	107
59	Argand burner	108
60	Gaselier, Royal Pavilion, Brighton	111
61	Georgian 'door knocker' chandelier	111
62	Regency candle lantern	113
63	Marine lamp	117
64	Paraffin lamp	118
65	Fishtail gas burners	120
66	Gas table lamp	121
67	Installation at Cragside	125
68	Edwardian electrolier	127
69	Bronze boy	128
70	Rush holder	131
71	Double-pan crusie	131
72	Mayflower candlestick	132
73	Wood and metal chandelier	133
74	Governor's Office chandelier	135
75	Printing Office chandelier	135
76	Wythe House Lantern	136
77	Guard House lantern	136
78	Colonial candlesticks	137
79	Whale oil and camphene lamps	140
80	Adam style chandelier	141
81	English Empire bracket	142
82	Hitchcock lamp	143
83	Hanging lamp	144
84	Suite of lamps	145
85	Salon in New York	150
86	Electrolier	152

LINE DRAWINGS

Forms of Decoration	14
Appendix One: Changing Shapes:	
Candle Arms	154
Candle Sticks	156
Oil Lamps	158
Gas Lamps	160
Appendix Two:	
Matching Fittings with Furniture	162

Acknowledgement for Illustrations

Ivan M. Allen Ltd., 30; Brighton Corporation, 60; E. Bruschi, Italy, 84; Craft House, Williamsburgh, Virginia U.S.A., 72, 74, 75, 76, 77, 78; Cecil Ern & Co., Ltd., 15, 33, 34, 35, 42, 43; Dernier & Hamlyn & Co. Ltd., 17, 25, 45, 46, 48, 49, 68, 73, 86; Homeshade & Co. Ltd., 21; Impex & Co. Ltd., 29; "Crown Copyright", Science Museum, London, 1, 2, 12, 22, 39, 40, 59, 63, 64, 66, 67, 70, 79, 82, 85; "Lent to Science Museum, London, by Gas Light & Coke Company", 71; Photo, Science Museum, London, 31; Mr. Argante Tipaldi, 7; "Crown Copyright", Victoria & Albert Museum, London, 4, 5, 8, 9, 11, 13, 24, 41, 50, 53, 54, 58, 81; Reproduced by permission of the Trustees of the Wallace Collection, 18, 19, 23, 26; Harland and Wolff, Belfast, 69; Author's Collection, 3, 6, 10, 14, 16, 27, 28, 32, 36, 37, 38, 44, 47, 51, 52, 55, 56, 57, 61, 62, 80, 81.

Acknowledgements

In order of priority I must thank Mr. Ivan M. Allen and Mr. Argante Tipaldi at whose suggestion this work was commenced, and my wife on whose insistence it was completed – five years later.

Major contributions to research into early lighting devices were provided by exhibits and works of reference in the British Museum, the Science Museum and the Victoria and Albert Museum; and a special mention is due to Williamsburgh Restoration Inc., for their contribution to the Colonial section of the American chapter.

In seeking suppliers of original or reproduction fittings, it is of interest to observe that almost all the historical periods are represented in the lighting departments of London's departmental stores, both Harrods of Knightsbridge and Selfridges of Oxford Street being popular venues of lighting consultants and their clients. The management of these great stores have been most co-operative in allowing me to compare their designs with the descriptions of those appearing in this book.

Illustrations are a major contribution to the success of the accompanying text, and this fact is thankfully acknowledged in the list of illustrations.

STANLEY WELLS
London 1974.

"The artificial production and supply of light during the absence of the sun, unquestionably holds a distinguished rank among the most important arts of civilised life."

Frederick Accum, 1815.

A SELECTION OF TRADITIONAL DESIGNS

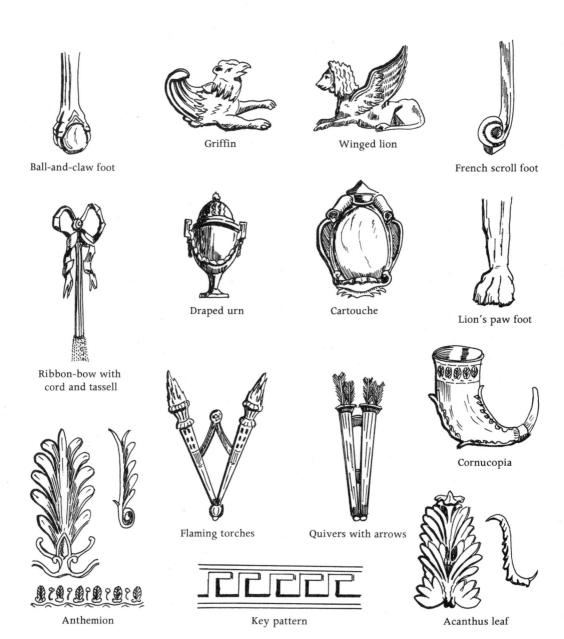

Ball-and-claw foot

Griffin

Winged lion

French scroll foot

Ribbon-bow with cord and tassell

Draped urn

Cartouche

Lion's paw foot

Cornucopia

Anthemion

Flaming torches

Quivers with arrows

Key pattern

Acanthus leaf

Introduction

Deep in the obscurity of pre-historic time, when man's first light was the day and his first heat was the sun, the discovery of fire-making at once provided an independent source of both heat and light for his future convenience; and in the dawn of intelligent invention he soaked a bundle of twigs in animal fat to make his first torch.

As his attention became increasingly occupied with the safety and mobility of artificial light, Stone Age man fashioned for himself the first lamp; a hollowed stone to contain fat and a moss wick, the principle of which was destined to survive unchallenged for centuries to come.

Evidence of the time involved in the evolution of the lamp has been provided by the discovery of one made from sandstone some 20,000 years ago, while a number of hollow stones discovered in caves at Lascaux, France, and recognised as primitive lamps, were estimated to be about 15,000 years old.

For those who dwelt alongside the lakes or within reach of the sea, Nature provided fish from which to extract oil, and shells in which to burn it. The fusus shell, for example, lends itself readily to adaption as an oil-burning lamp, as it has a deep font and a natural upturned spout for use as a wick channel.

It could he held steady by embedding it in a base of clay, or it could be suspended by securing a thong around its centre, and many a cave and mud hut was illuminated by this simple device.

Lamps such as these have been discovered in the Orkney Islands, while further evidence of their use is to be seen in the ancient Shell Temple in Margate, Kent. There, in the chamber which contains the altar, one can see two large conch shells set in the corners at the junction of wall and ceiling.

Before the east wall was damaged by bombing in 1944, there were four of these shells, which, in ancient times, were charged with oil and wick to light the chamber as worshippers gathered to pay homage to their gods.

Fish, birds and animals were all good sources of burnable oils, and long ago the inhabitants of Vancouver Island, Canada, would catch and store quantities of oily salmonoid fish to provide their lighting requirements for the winter, the dried fish being impaled on a spike and the oil being ignited at the mouth.

In the Shetland Islands, the oily stormy petrel served as a torch, with its feet embelled in clay to give it stability, and a fibre wick threaded through the beak into the interior.

Animal and fish oils were also burned in the sea shells which were collected in profusion, not only for their edible contents but also for their functional use as oil fonts, and throughout many centuries the shell had so much become associated with use as a lamp, that later generations reproduced its likeness in alabaster, stone and clay; and it is known that alabaster lamps carved in the form of shells were used around 2600 B.C.

These curious lighting devices are the ancestors of the Roman hand lamp, the Egyptian saucer, and many kinds of lamps from Persia and Turkey, all of which provided an essential service throughout the several centuries during which technical improvements were impossible, and when only variation of design contributed to the appeal of the product.

Little from the distant past has survived the destructions of man and time, and our knowledge is dependent upon the discovery of relics, the scrutiny of manuscripts and illustrations, old inventories, official records, and the application of logical deduction to what we find.

There are relics like those excavated from the ruins of Herculaneum and Pompeii, amongst which we discover the lamps that were actually in use when the great Vesuvius erupted and buried them all in a sea of lava and volcanic ash.

There are relics like the little bronze lamp excavated from the old market in Athens, and believed to be about 1,500 years old; and there are relics like the tall alabaster lamps found in the tomb of King Tutankhamun.

Engravings, wood-cuts and prints have confirmed the ancient use in many countries of fire-splints, rush-lights and float-lamps, and there are informative observations in diaries, books and documents which describe the style of candlesticks and chandeliers.

Our earliest written reference to a sophisticated form of lighting device is to be found in the Bible, in the Book of Exodus (900–1000 B.C.), in which Moses receives the Tablets of the Law on Mount Sinai, and is commanded to build and furnish a tabernacle.

Excerpts from the text give us an insight to the specific instructions concerning the first sacred lamp:

"Thou shalt make an ark of acacia wood . . . thou shalt make a candlestick and the lamps to give light. And thou shalt make a candlestick of pure gold; of beaten work shall the candlestick be made; his shaft, and his branches, his bowls, his knops, and his flowers, shall be of the same . . . And thou shalt make seven lamps thereof; and they shall light the lamps thereof. . . ."

Moses was even told how to fashion the candlestick and it was in this way:

"And six branches shall come out of the sides of it; three branches of the candlestick out of the one side, and three branches of the candlestick out of the other side."

Because, at the time of translation, there was no English equivalent for this seven light lamp-stand, it was loosely termed a 'candlestick', but it was, in fact, an elaborate stand bearing oil cups at the end of each branch, a deduction borne out by the text in Exodus verse 37 which states: ". . . the pure candlestick with the lamps thereof . . . and all the vessels thereof, and the oil for light."

This lamp is, of course, the Menorah, which has remained as a symbolic lamp of the synagogue ever since.

The development of early lighting devices, and their adoption by communities along the trade routes of the world, depended more on their suitability for everyday needs and to the kind of fuel available in the locality than on their visual appeal.

It could have taken as long as five years for a little glass lamp to be taken from Venice to France, and another five before it found a favourable buyer in England. En route, its likeness could have been reproduced by craftsmen in several other countries, and there might have been variations made in the design by the more creative workers amongst them, for which reason it is sometimes difficult to identify an article as having originated from one particular source.

Only by familiarity with original pieces does one acquire the expertise to recognise the genuinely old from the recent reproduction, and only by diligent study of period furnishings can one acquire the art of matching the furnishings and lighting fittings for a given period.

Each nation and each generation of craftsmen contributes something of its own towards inspiration in others, and distinctive designs have continuity throughout the reproduction of traditional styles.

Renaissance art, having established its roots in Italy, matured in the sophistication of Western Europe, only to be delivered back to the land of its birth a century or so later, displaying the embellishments that it had collected on the way.

A collector may have to ask himself if a certain silver candlestick is of Italian manufacture, or an English copy of the Italian style, or even if it is a Russian interpretation of an English candlestick based on Italian design; and the answer is provided by his knowledge of local workmanship, and of the evolution of decorative motifs used for embellishment.

In this way, a future generation of antiquarians may look back on our period, and in their wisdom, declare that this chromium-plated electrolier was made by Clarklite in 1974, or that this crystal fitting was sold by Focus Lighting in 1975: at which the uninitiated will marvel at their skill.

In looking for clues to origin and period, we must first look at the overall shape of the article, then for the 'sign-language' of ornamental design – recognisable patterns which are distinguishable by their individuality throughout centuries of development – and by means of keen deduction we may arrive at the style, origin, date, designer and value.

We may recall that the ornamentation devised by the Greeks and Egyptians was readily adopted by the Romans, who in turn contributed modifications which, centuries afterwards, inspired the designers of the French Empire to reproduce their likeness for the Court of Napoleon.

The key to understanding the great periods of furnishing design lies in the recognition of the successive order of Gothic, Renaissance, Baroque, Rococo and Neo-Classic, all of which are discussed in this book.

Although there are several comprehensive collections of old lighting devices in private and state museums all over the world, because of their bulk on the one hand and their rarity on the other, lighting fittings are not collected after the manner of pictures, guns and coins, and so much was disposed of during 'modernisation' from about 1885 onwards, that most of the so-called 'old' fittings in circulation are reproductions dating no further back than the early 1900s.

Many of the 'antique' table lamps currently in circulation were originally ornaments such as cassolettes, clock ornaments and figureines, which have been adapted for use as electric table lamps by the simple device of fitting a stem and lamp holder.

While most of these pieces are signed and sometimes dated, the signatures are confined to the object as an orament and not to its status as a light fitting, and they cannot be considered as antique lamps. Therefore, the signatures, as significant as they may be to a collector of antiques, are unimportant to the lighting historian, although their association with a given style could be of value at another time.

Because of their long-standing practice of marking their wares, the work of silversmiths, goldsmiths and pewterers is easily identified with the aid of an appropriate manual of trade marks.

Otherwise there are few lighting fittings which bear signatures, and even fewer bearing signatures of significance to us today, since we cannot always be certain whether the marks belonged to the designer, the caster, the finisher or the owner. However, as our story is more concerned with the development of lighting and the characteristic forms of period styles, we need not concern ourselves too deeply with collector's items or antique pieces, although everything mentioned in this book must fall into one category or the other.

Through the media of the following chapters, the reader may learn to relate traditional lighting designs to their specific periods, and to complement period furnishings with appropriate lighting devices, for such knowledge is as essential to the architect as to the antiquarian; as valuable to the lighting engineer as to the furniture salesman; as necessary to the renovation of a stately home as to the introduction of traditional taste to the suburban villa, and is integral with the daily lives of all who are engaged about the business of interior decoration.

In the treasure chests of the past the observant eye will discover much of beauty and a great deal of pleasure in its pursuit of the golden days of lighting.

CHAPTER ONE

Italy

The disintegration of the Roman Empire, the shattering effects of barbaric domination and almost continuous war, led not only to the deterioration of civil order but was responsible also for the decline in sciences and arts which encouraged the period we know as the Dark Ages.

Within fifty years of the Fall of the Empire little remained of the administration and skills which had been developed by the Romans, and even earlier by the Etruscans. Devices for producing light were few and purely functional in their own crude way, and remained undeveloped since the days when Rome was lighted by burning braziers and huge oil dishes, most of which now lay buried in the ruins of their buildings and civilisation, or embalmed in the erupted lava of Vesuvius.

The common lamp was of baked clay, with a wick which would frequently burn badly or messily (Plate 1). Many of these little hand lamps had provided the light by which the early Christians found their way to meeting places in the catacombs beneath Rome, and for that reason, and also

because some of them bear religious symbols, they are often called 'Christian's Lamps'.

More rare, and infrequently made by the diminishing communities of metal workers, the form of the Roman lamp was reproduced and improved upon in bronze or brass, being fitted with a wick and a protective lid. These were the typical Roman lamps of antiquity which are still made familiar to modern generations in the

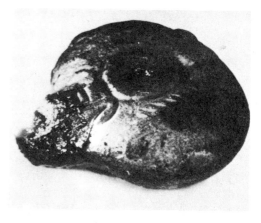

1   Roman hand lamp, First Century.

beautiful form of the Aladdin's lamp of folk-tale fame.

When it was necessary to increase the amount of light even the addition of salt to the oil contributed little towards a brighter light, and lamps were also made with multiple spouts to fulfil the need. The Romans used wick-spout lamps which provided several 'kettle' spouts arranged around a central oil font. A wick threaded through the length of each spout and down into the font allowed the oil to seep up to the opening where it was ignited. These lamps were suspended from wall brackets, standard tripods or ceiling hooks by means of thongs or chains.

Some of the lamps were plainly made, some were coloured, and others were decorated with moulded or carved garlands, human masks or animals heads (Plate 2). But as the old designs of the shattered Empire fell into disuse through lack of native endeavour to reproduce them, trade with the Orient and Near East introduced articles of foreign manufacture which superseded those of the Italians.

In the dim light of the dark ages, pierced metal mosque lamps found their way into Christian churches; lamps which had once been reserved for the sanctuary burned in domestic surroundings, and a profusion of outside influences infiltrated into the principal towns.

There is no telling for how long this state of affairs might have continued had it not been for the struggle to maintain the remnants of the Eastern Empire in Byzantium, where scholars and men of dedicated purpose kept alive the skills of their inherited culture; unobstrusively and almost unknown to the outside world, until

2 *Hanging lamp from Pompeii, First Century.*

the bitter invasion which deprived them of their sanctuary.

When in 1453 the Turks attacked and overran the city of Byzantium, subsequently Constantinople, the Eastern Roman Empire collapsed, and in so doing closed the era which we know as the Byzantine Period (328–1453).

The great cultural society of scholars, architects and engineers which had flourished in the last surviving corner of the crumbling Empire, now took refuge in Italy, where, in the course of time, their knowledge of the Classic arts became recognised as an unparalleled revelation of past achievements in design and craftsmanship. This is the point in history at which began the 'new birth' – the *Renaissance.*

During the fifteen centuries which separate the use of fine Roman lamps from the rediscovery of the Classic arts in the Renaissance, a great many lighting fittings must have perished, and all that remains to excite our curiosity are fragments of small lamps and pictorial evidence of the beauty that must have been the glory of Rome. When excavations in the hills around Rome brought to light archaeological treasures of a thousand years previous, and revealed a way of life which had long faded from history, men of learning and invention stood aghast at the possibility of engineering the re-birth of a by-gone era, and great bronze candelabra, splendid lanterns, and exquisite terra-cotta hand lamps, were among the items that inspired new thought and a revolution in design.

Prominent artists and others whose opinions were respected by wealthy patrons, quickly recognised the potential of adopting the principles of ancient design for the foundations of a new Italy, and lost no time in applying their brilliant skills to developing fresh ideas based on the reconstructed past.

Leonardo da Vinci spread the news across Europe, Raphael, Michelangelo and Cellini added their individual genius to copying, modifying and improving upon the ancient designs, and these soon became the templates for establishing a new style in living and in an appreciation of the arts.

The great candelabra designed by Raphael are still treasured in Italy, and many of the ewers and jugs made by Cellini have been copied in modern times for the pleasure of those who love beautiful things.

But anciently there was no industry for making lighting fittings, and only the wealthy possessed anything in the least elaborate after the fall of the Empire, and the passing centuries provided nothing more than the most rudimentary forms of lighting device.

The use of candles was common as early as the Sixth Century but it is evident that lamps were more convenient and probably more generally used as olive oil for burning was more readily available than the fat for candles, and in any event, the reasonably even distribution of daylight throughout any twenty-four hour period raised no great demand for artificial light. The little hand lamp, the torch holder and the lantern sufficed for all general-purpose lighting, and even these had their foundations in the cultures of Egypt and the Near East.

In both Greece and Rome, pottery lamps were used by the peasants and less prosperous merchants, and for all the extra luxury enjoyed by the wealthy classes, the best that could be done for their lamps was to produce them in bronze and to adorn them with decoration, for there was no means of making them burn more brightly or less smokily.

Study shows that although similar in principle, lighting devices were not the same in all countries as there was little trade in this type of product, most of the lamps and splints being locally made and sold in exchange for other domestic commodities, but it is reasonable to assume that almost everyone, or at least every family group, needed and owned a lighting device of some kind. Design, such as it was, had to be suited to the type of fuel available for burning, and this varied according to the natural products of the land. For example, the clay lamps burned a liquid fuel such as olive oil or nut oil, and was consequently more suited to use in Mediterranean countries, whereas in areas of Central Europe, where only animal fat could be used, a form of shallow grease pan served as a lamp, and these were more generally used than candles, although not so frequently as fire splints or rushlights.

In the north, as in the northernmost territories of all countries, the longer hours of darkness and the early twilight encouraged a more general use of artificial light by which to continue the affairs of the household. There was invariably a meal to prepare, clothes to wash and mending to be done, as well as spinning and baking and the usual pursuits of family life.

Candles were scarce and tedious to make. Often there was not enough oil for the lamp; but the people cut finely split slivers of pine in which the natural pitch burned well and brightly in spite of the messy shedding of molten pitch and charred wood. Before splint holders were devised, the burning splint, sometimes up to three feet long, was held either in the mouth or in a band around the head so that it was possible to move about the house keeping the hands free for more useful occupations.

As these conditions prevailed throughout most of the world, but with native modifications occasioned by the demands of the environment, we shall not spend much time discussing these primitive devices since they are more suited to a separate study, and our real intention is to trace the course of the more significant pieces that contribute to the later decorative periods. Not everyone was poor and there were craftsmen whose skill and dedication could be employed for special assignments, and because of this not all lighting fittings were simple or roughly made.

Large candlesticks and hanging fittings for churches were particularly in evidence as the more ritualistic ceremonies of the Christian era began to demand a more exclusive and flamboyant style of decoration and furnishing. Hanging lamps in the sanctuary were commonplace in the Ninth Century, and often took their place with the Gothic iron hanging candlehoops from France.

Although it is common practice to class Italian antiques and architecture as Gothic if their dates fall between the Thirteenth and Fifteenth Centuries, the Gothic in Italy was largely influenced by her inherent appreciation of the classic arts, and one finds a traditional blending of Gothic and Classic throughout her art forms.

Nevertheless, while it is generally considered that the Gothic was more at home in France, England and Spain, the craft of manipulation in Italian ironwork is conspicuous for delicacy, form and decorative beauty, every piece worked lovingly so as to resemble a lace-like treatment (Plate 3). Torches, cressets and lantern brackets vied powerfully for recognition among banner sockets, railings, balconies, gates and window shutters.

From early times, in large areas of the mosque or church, a large diameter iron hoop would be suspended on chains, and had fitted around its circumference a number of small oil bowls, these being made of iron, glass or precious metal

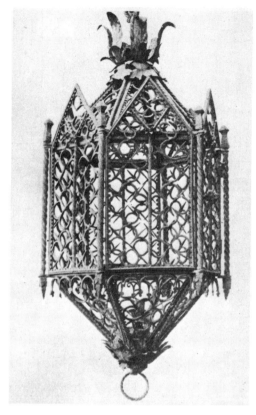

3 *Iron Gothic lantern, Fifteenth Century.*

introduction of a floating disc or triangle of metal which almost overed the oil's surface and was supported by corks, helped to keep the dirt and insects at bay.

Bowls were made with several spouts hammered around their rim in the case of metal, or moulded into those made of glass. A wick laid in each spout with its end trailing in the oil, soaking it up towards the air. Sometimes a metal lid was placed inside the rim of the bowl to hold the wick in place and to protect the oil from foreign bodies. The wicks, when ignited from a long taper, formed a pretty pattern of dancing flame. In this simple device is seen the basis of all old oil lamps, the principle being known since before Biblical times, but was not to be perfected for nearly seven hundred years. Small, multi-wick lamps could be suspended from wall brackets or mounted on a stem for standing on a table. A boat-shaped version with a single wick channel and an open oil reservoir served as a hand lamp for personal use after dark. Most of these were made of baked clay, but the more costly ones were of bronze and decorated with simple motifs.

The earliest pottery lamps were a simple shallow saucer with a wick channel or open lip in which the wick was laid, and these were handed on from the Egyptians to the Romans.

Curious and beautiful ware from the Orient and Western Continents had long established the Saracenic touch or the enterprise of fashion conscious Central Europeans in most of Italy's designs, and not the least among these many items were the candlesticks produced in the Netherlands village of Dinant between the Eleventh and Fourteenth Centuries. These designs,

according to the availability of the materials or the requirements of the priests.

Mostly these little lamps were 'float lamps', that is to say the wick was threaded through a thin disc which was floated on the surface of the oil. Larger float lamps were made of blown glass bowls suspended on wires or chain, and these were known as 'Italian lamps' for several centuries.

But whatever the size of the oil font, the flame was small and insects and dust particles were apt to form an unpleasant scum on the surface which often clogged the wick and extinguished the flame. The usually made in brass, copper or bronze, consisted of a candlestick delicately decorated with grotesques, naturalistic and animal forms; often gilded or otherwise decorated with *champlevé* or *cloissonné* enamelling, both techniques being ably adopted by the Italians in their native reproduction works.

Plainer designs in baluster forms were introduced as altar candlesticks or were tall enough to stand on the floor, and were so widely used that they are often classed as Flemish-Italian candlesticks.

Churches, palaces and public buildings displayed large bronze Romanesque style candelabra, while for the less important occasions the *Lucerna* was generally to be found.

According to needs, this oil-burning lamp was obtainable in various sizes. There was the small hand lamp suspended from a chain, and a larger multi-wick lamp could be hung from a wall bracket or from a chain attached to a hook in the ceiling. It was also made on a tall stem for standing on the floor, or on a shorter stem for table use.

In the latter years of the Fifteenth Century, both oil and candle were in general use. Indoors, servants held rush torches close to the table at meal times. The small and large candlesticks sufficed for the bed chamber and the corridor, while multiple arrays achieved the best possible display of light for the great hall.

Out of doors an occasional post lantern gave scant light for the night watch or the infrequent traveller, although some streets and archways were provided with wall mounted iron *cressets* (Plate 4) in which was burned coils of rope soaked in pitch.

Overall, the selection of lighting devices

4 Braccio cresset, *Sixteenth Century.*

in everyday use was limited to the purely functional needs of the people, and the individual pieces were identified by these names:

lucerna	Bronze or brass Roman lamp.
lampada	oil lamp.
lampione	standard or post lantern.
lanterna	hanging lantern.
candeliere	small candlestick.

candelabro large candlestick.

corona 'crown of light', a multi-light fitting for oil lamps or candles.

torciere floor standard for candles.

The *torciere* was the ancestor of our present day floor standard lamp. In the Fourteenth Century this was a simple iron rod mounted on a tripod base, having had its top filed to a point to take the candle. In later models an iron hoop, or square gallery, was supported by brackets on the central shaft, sometimes at the top, sometimes half-way down the shaft, and this bore the prickets or sockets for the candles. When lighted it resembled a brilliant, flickering crown of light and so earned the name *corona*.

Development of these floor standards resulted in handsome scrolled feet, knopped stems and applied acanthus scrolls as ornament, surviving into the Seventeenth Century as the *torciere di ferro* (Plate 5).

Candelabro of the Fifteenth Century were tall and beautiful, being carved from Tuscan walnut and heavily decorated with Renaissance motifs, polychromed (coloured) or polished. In the high Renaissance model (Plate 6), the central shaft rested on a three-cornered plinth raised on lions paws and overhung with scrolls and acanthus decoration. The shaft progressed upwards to the candle socket in baluster forms of urn, ball, vase and bun-shaped components, and was further decorated with rams heads, swags of oak leaf, bunches of grapes and grotesques. They were made not only of wood but also of bronze, silver, alabaster and, more rarely, of gold; the sizes ranging from about seventeen inches to eight feet.

A more restrained treatment produced a tall candlestick with the basic bun and urn

5 Torciere di ferro, *Sixteenth Century.*

6 *Renaissance* candelabro, *Fifteenth Century.*

known as 'Florentine candlesticks'. Some bases bear the artists signature, and two skillful craftsmen who added their names to notable Renaissance pieces, were Riccio and Pollaninolo.

The human form – in the shape of angels, sirens, cherubs and cupids – figures prominently in the decoration of more elaborate candlesticks. Cupids (*amorini*) mounted on gold or silver plinths, held aloft foliated candle sockets, or supported slim shafts topped by a pricket and drip-pan. Cherubs (*putti*) mounted on gold or silver bases, held floral garlands, or cornucopias with a socket for the candle inside the opening (Plate 7). Not all were made of metal. Many were of carved wood, some of alabaster and some of stone. Even today reproductions cast in plaster are eagerly sought as principal decorations for domestic use.

Angels were cast in full figure with wings aspread, and holding aloft a shaft and candle socket in each delicately chiselled hand.

Lanterns were made of wood, iron or bronze, and came in various sizes depending upon their purpose. They were made as bracket lights (*braccio*) with ornamental brackets, and were often highly coloured. For light they housed either float lamps or candles. They were also mounted on poles (*lampione*) to light the streets at night or to carry in processions.

Lanterns, made of iron or lead with glass or horn windows, were splendidly gilded and hung on stairways, under arches and along galleries. They had window-type openings which allowed access to the chamber which contained either candle, pitch-rope or wick-in-oil lamps.

shapes set on a scrolled plinth standing on three squat feet. Leafwork and scrolls decorate the shaft, almost obscuring the more formal groundwork.

Candeliere, varying in height from a few inches to three feet or so, repeated the designs of the larger models, although some are extremely simple in carved wood and either fluted and polished or smooth and painted. Reproductions are generally

7 Cherub with cornucopia.

The early Renaissance lantern tapers towards the top instead of towards the bottom, as is the case with Moorish and Spanish lanterns, but later models are rectangular and taper towards the bottom.

Throughout the course of furnishing development the sign language of decorative devices serves as a guide to attributing dates and designers' names to objects of art, and those devices used by the ancient Empire were now restored to prominence in the Renaissance. Classic forms used on lanterns and candlesticks included griffins, sea gods, medallions, shells, sphinxes, dragons, satyrs, lions' paws, eagles, nymphs, male and female figures, cupids, cherubs, and a profusion of acanthus leaf and floral garlands.

The Sixteenth Century had numerous hanging lamps in bronze, brass, silver and wood, and of these the sanctuary lamp is probably the most interesting for its ancestory because, in principle, the evolution of the hanging chandelier is traced back to those old lamps which gave meagre light in both Christian and pagan places of worship as early as the First Century.

In the hanging lamp, a large silver or bronze bowl was suspended from the roof on three or four chains, or on twisted rope. In earliest times the decoration was beaten into the metal by hammer and in later models was delicately chased and cut (Plate 8). Less elaborate models were made in brass or glass.

Typical of the sanctuary lamp is the vase shape of the font, diminishing downwards with the aid of ball- and baluster-shaped members which terminate in a pineapple or pomegranate finial with, perhaps, a ring attached. The more elaborate members of the family are decorated by *repoussé* work or chasing.

The most important development arising from these old lamps was the *lampadario* which had candle arms with sockets fitted around the circumference of the font so that both oil and candles could be burned at the same time.

Exactly when this sire of all chandeliers came into being is not yet known but by

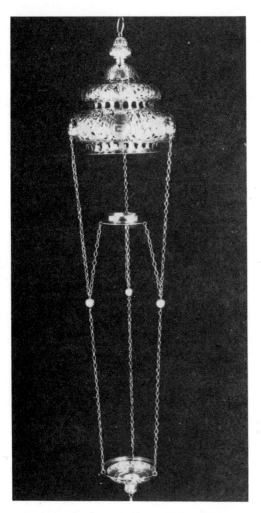

8 Lampada, *Sanctuary lamp, Sixteenth Century.*

clusion that chandeliers were already well known by that time.

Although Italy now held a position of authority in the most influential art circles of the awakening world, many of her lighting fittings still came from distant parts; candlesticks from the Netherlands, Gothic lanterns from Spain, lamps from Persia, and glass candelabra from Bohemia found their place among the decorative treasures of the land. But by the mid-Sixteenth Century the Renaissance revolution was being modified by new lines of thought being injected into architecture and art by Michelangelo, and from these freshly conceived ideas was born the Baroque period of architecture and design which was destined to influence Italy and other Western European countries until the Eighteenth Century.

Because of their durability, the use of different kinds of metal and wood had been preferred to the extensive use of glass, especially in connection with lighting fittings, but glass was by no means ignored by the craftsmen and designers of the day.

Glass making to the Venetians was a legacy left by the Romans who had learned their glass making from the Syrians and Alexandrians; and as appreciation of the craft developed in the hands of glass craftsmen and came under the patronage of wealthy citizens, many beautiful designs were born.

The Venetian glass chandelier, *lumiere di cristallo,* is generally accepted as being the ancestor of all glass chandeliers, and dates from the Seventeenth Century. As we have already seen this is not the first use of glass in connection with illumination, as Persian glass bowls were used as lamps in the

the process of elimination, and having regard to the availability of candles, it would seem that a broadly cast guess would put its introduction as being between the Third and Ninth Centuries. The export of bronze chandeliers from the Netherlands is thought to have begun during the Twelfth/Thirteenth Centuries, and their sophisticated design leads to the con-

Eleventh Century, and a simple oil font with floating wick was used in mosques as early as A.D. 300. But the assembled components of centre shaft, candle arms, candle sockets and artistic decoration of the whole piece, was indeed entirely Italian.

Some of these magnificent fittings were a riot of swirling, exfoliating glass leaves, petals and garlands, in coloured and clear glass, and by the middle of the Seventeenth Century had been introduced into many homes as features to be admired and even envied.

The late Seventeenth and early Eighteenth Centuries, saw the introduction of crystal decorations in the form of pendants of various designs, which included peardrops, star-drops, marguerites, prisms and spheres. Swags and pendants made of glass were hung on all types of lighting fitting, including those of bronze, brass, iron and silver. Eventually a basic design evolved from a profusion of ideas, and we find the solution being established in the form of a metal framework of cage-like construction, which when draped with crystals resembled a beautiful glass tree with its petals and flowers springing from all over its stem. It was a design which soon found favour in the glassworks of Bohemia and France.

Mirror-backed sconces, *specchi colle lumiere,* were made to complement the centre pieces, while at the same time the French taste for handsomely framed mirrors with candle branches was introduced in the style of Louis XIV. This kind of exchange in fashionable designs was becoming quite common, and naturally encouraged an intermingling of styles.

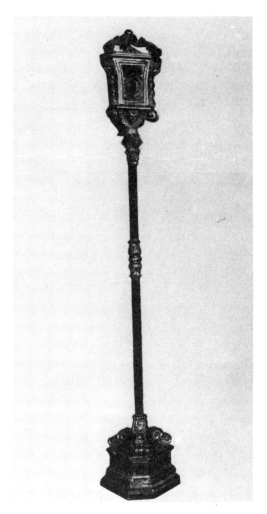

9 Lampione *in French style, c.1700.*

Evidence of this admixture of native and foreign components is shown in the exquisite workmanship of a pole lantern (*lampione*) of carved and gilded wood which is dated about 1700, and is in the style of Louis XIV. The pole is covered by red velvet, being interrupted in the middle by gilded acanthus ornament, and it stands delicately on three scrolled feet in a

10   Lumière *with flowers, Eighteenth Century.*

stepped wooden plinth of polished walnut. The lantern, with blown glass windows, is bold with Baroque carving, and is supported on the top of the pole by winged cherubs heads. At the top of the lantern its smoke bell is well disguised by bold carving; and the top rests on a woman's head at each corner (Plate 9).

Rare and beautiful in Italian lighting designs are those fittings which are delicately fashioned of thin wrought-iron scroll work, overlaid with flowers and leaves, and skilfully hand painted (Plate 10).

A lovely touch of artistry allows for the addition of a single figure or group of figures in the Capo di Monte porcelain; the fitting taking the name *Lumiere Capo di Monte,* and becoming widely popular during the first half of the Eighteenth Century.

Most, if not all, of the originals are either in museums or are in private ownership, but there are many reproductions right through to the present day. The originals, and those made up to about the end of the Nineteenth Century, have solid arms, but those after the advent of electricity may have tubular arms through which the electric flex is threaded to the centre body. It is, on the other hand, possible that a reproduction may have the flex attached to the framework by means of wire, and only knowledge of current production techniques will enable the student to identify it as ancient or modern. Dresden and other porcelains were used in similar manner, and such work was especially noteworthy in France.

After the commencement of the Renaissance, over 250 years passed before fresh revelations renewed the impetus which had all but settled; Rome had again been rebuilt on the ashes and rubble of the ancient city, and the new buildings which had been recreated in the classic style had given way to the theatrical power of the Baroque.

Ornaments, copied from the treasures so far excavated from the ancient ruins had been widely spread throughout the world, especially in the West. Both Rome and Florence were centres of learning and example. Men of talent and education came to look and to learn for themselves from the fountain of knowledge which was Italy, for the news travelled slowly in those days, and when Italy was enjoying her Baroque, England was struggling with her interpretation of the Renaissance.

But if the technicians and patrons of the past had been inspired by those early discoveries, there were more startling events to come; events which would wring from the very shrouds of antiquity such treasures of design and culture that the entire world would henceforth derive its standards of traditional design from the grave-yards of the past.

In 1706, during the deepening of a well, relics were found under the surface of the ground which lead to the partial excavation of the site, and there, from depths of fourteen to one hundred feet below the village, and below the lava and ash of the long-ago eruptions of Vesuvius, lay the ancient city of Herculaneum, not known since its macabre embalmment in A.D. 79.

Statues, ornaments, pictures, oil lamps and candle holders were found among the treasures of antiquity as the ground was carefully dug away from the ruined buildings, and much more has been removed from the site since that momentous first dig.

Once a popular resort of the Romans, the similarly tragic city of Pompeii had also been buried in those volcanic eruptions, and excavations during 1748 brought to light many treasures and revealed parts of temples, houses and city walls which have since been disinterred.

These relics of the First Century included many small lamps for domestic use and great tripod standards for communal use, only a fraction of the wealth of discoveries given up by the generous earth to kindle the flame of interest which brought Italy alive with the revival which was afterwards called Neo-Classicism.

The most important influence on style and design of the new era was the publication by Piranesi, a Venetian, whose detailed drawings of classic decoration and ornament formed the basic for all other design-

ers to follow. But as it happened on this occasion, the finer principles of the newly found arts were more expertly interpreted in France than in the homeland, and as France had now become the trend-setting centre of Europe, the neo-classic revival journeyed there to receive its embellishments before returning to Italy for native approval: and Italy proved to be as ready to take to her heart the artistic offerings of her neighbours as those of her own countrymen. In this way she absorbed, with genuine pleasure, the French styles of the Directoire and the Empire, the principles of which are still best studied in France.

Even so, the Italians continued to demonstrate their own creativeness,

11   Candeliere Veneziano, *1862.*

especially in the glass art for which they were world famous. Most individual of Italian glass candlesticks are the Venetian glass candelabrum called *Candeliero Veneziano* (Plate 11), a confection of ornamental flower-like shapes in coloured glass that is of outstanding merit in the field of glass making in the Eighteenth Century.

Although unsuited to domestic collections, such pieces are a frequent source of admiration in museums. They are, however, of lesser value if they have suffered the indignity of having been converted for electricity.

When looking back over the lighting devices of several centuries, it becomes apparent that the most long-lasting, widely copied and eminently functional lamp was the *Lucerna,* a heavy brass table lamp which had survived from early times until late in the Nineteenth Century (Plate 12). A central stem arises from a circular foot and carries a shallow lid-covered oil font which is adjustable along the length of the column. Three or more wick spouts project from the sides of the font in duplicate of the old hanging lamps found in Pompeii. A metal shield hooks into a bracket just under the carrying ring and this serves as an eye shield when reading or working. Attached to chains hanging below the font are forceps, spike, wick-box and extinguisher. Copied all over the world, it is often found in antique shops and collections, not only produced in miniature, but also in giant, floor-standing models which must have been used in public buildings or large halls.

The background for all the unrivalled beauty described in this chapter is typically gay and Italian. Carved and painted furniture with rich upholstery; buttons,

12 Lucerna, *Eighteenth Century.*

fringes and tassels set against costly fabrics and floor coverings provided the colour and atmosphere for the interiors which came alive with the light from lamps and candles as twilight fell upon the land.

Here then, it is prudent to take our departure, remembering Italy at her traditional best, and having established her as the source of inspiration which provided the Western world with a reason for including her in the Grand Tour of elegant education.

In passing it is worth our attention to note how persistently the fountain of Italian design has continued to inspire centuries of designers and craftsmen right through to the present day.

CHAPTER TWO

France

The geographical position of France, or Gaul as it was called until the Ninth Century, encouraged her to absorb the artistic and artisian skills of her more enterprising neighbours, and from far and near the travellers came to sell their wares and to introduce their cultures. But owing to the primitive and severe conditions that existed in the northern regions the traders were not anxious to press their attentions beyond the profitable southern routes, so there is little of interest in the way of decorative arts except, perhaps, for a local industry in metal bangles, brooches and simple candlesticks.

On the other hand where ships sailed on the Mediterranean, bearing travellers and traders from distant lands, the culture of the southern territories was enriched by the influences of Byzantium, Italy and the Orient; and the ironwork of Spain in filtrated into those parts bordering the Pyrenees, a circumstance which ensured a generous supply of iron lanterns, gates, balconies and lighting fittings.

The Romanesque period from 700 to 1100 included the combining of Christian and Roman art, after which the Gothic period from 1108 to 1515 influenced art forms until the arrival of the Renaissance from Italy during the reign of Louis XIII in the Sixteenth Century.

As with other countries, there was no industry for manufacturing lighting devices, they came by necessity from the hands of those best suited to working in the materials available, and the crudest hanging fittings were devised from a block of wood into which spikes were stuck to provide candle holders, the whole unit being suspended from a hook. Therefore, the majority of early lighting fittings were simple in design and functional in purpose.

The old Roman hand lamp, used in Gaul since the Roman invasion of 58 B.C., had been handed on from one generation to the next, and they, conscious only of its utilitarian function, saw no reason to vary or redesign it.

In the north, the difficulty of keeping the oil thin enough for absorption by the wick was further aggravated by the poor heat conductivity of the lamp, and this problem had to be solved by making a lamp that was more suited to colder climates and was able to burn the fat which was more abundantly available than oil.

The lamp in Gaul existed for the majority as the simple clay wick-spout lamp of antiquity; for the less poor it was more sophisticated in bronze, with lid, wick and handle, and probably served a wider population as a hanging oil pan known as the *candile*. This had its foreign counterparts in the Spanish *candil,* the Roman *velon,* and the Scottish *crusie* of roughly the same period. There was nothing special in its design, just a simple shallow iron pan with a pinched spout to hold the wick, and a vertical handle with a hook attachment for hanging. Where the wick-spout lamp was not in use, the pan lamp took its place.

By way of definition, the *pan lamp* is one in which the wick rests on the bottom of the pan instead of being supported on the edge, and the *wick spout* or *wick channel* lamp, popular in Scotland and other North Sea countries, has a deeper pan and a channel in which the wick rests. Both will burn fat, and they depend on using the heat from the flame to maintain the pan at a high enough temperature to liquify the fat.

Far Eastern influence, which had introduced the urn and ball shapes of the baluster stem candlestick into Holland and Italy in the Seventh Centry, was known in Twelfth Century France in the form of iron or bronze chandeliers with removable scroll arms radiating around a solid central sphere. There was a simple, crudely made hanging fitting in which the upturned cone-shaped sockets served to catch the dripping tallow as well as to hold the candle. From this basic idea they developed the great, sophisticated models of the Fourteenth Century which have survived in principal to the present day.

Brightly painted iron chandeliers from England, mostly in the form of hoops or cross beams, were brought into France by the landowning English.

But probably the most remarkable absorption of external art is to be found in the candlesticks made in the Netherlands village of Dinant between the Eleventh and Fourteenth Centuries.

The curious form of these *chandeliers de dinanderie* is characterised by the low, squat base resting firmly on animals feet and incorporating vigorous forms of chimerical beasts, dragons, birds, floral arrangements, serpents, lions, elephants, grotesques and human figures, features which recall Romanesque or Near Eastern origin. They were imported in abundance and were subsequently copied and sold as French products, bearing signatures and inscriptions.

Other candlesticks were also made of ivory, brass, copper, bronze or enamel, and were often decorated with precious stones, just as in *dinanderie* work, and as this style is an important facet in early lighting designs, so the Twelfth Century hanging lights known as *coronas* are an important transition from bronze to wrought iron.

The Twelfth Century *coronas* were large and heavy, and made in bronze, silver or iron, mostly in gilt bronze, and were undecorated except for the marks of the hammer on the hoop and the drip pans, but during the reign of St. Louis (1226–70) a much lighter treatment was developed in all media. In particular during this time the wrought-iron workers achieved a degree of proficiency which enabled them to produce delicate and artistic forms which became distinctive of the period, avoiding the lacy patterns of Italy, being less strident than the Spanish, and more sophisticated than the English.

The *roue de fer* – wheel of iron, developed in size and accumulated various motifs as decoration throughout the Gothic period. Early models were made to hold either candles or lamps around the circumference of a hoop suspended on chain or linked rods. As a *lampier* with small oil cups it suited the warmer climate of the south, but for sheer beauty it was at its best when burning candles, and justly deserved its name – *couronne de lumière*.

A hanging fitting of the Fifteenth Century was built-up around a flat iron hoop suspended from an elaborate central shaft be means of three link rods. The drip pans were emphasised by an encircling band of scalloped edge, and bore either sockets or prickets. Between the posts which upheld the pans was scrollwork with a flower head design. Many of these chandeliers were brightly enamelled, and were sometimes decorated with gold leaf work, ivory or glass, and some had tassels hanging around the pans.

By the time of the Renaissance almost every type of lighting fitting had been given an individual name. Many had found their way across the border into Spain, and across the Channel into England (especially at the time of the Norman Conquest), and they were known by their French names throughout Europe, where local workmen sometimes copied and reproduced their likeness in native materials but with certain modifications which often enable us to identify the country of origin.

All candlesticks were called *chandeliers* and so the term was used to include everything that held candles. Similarly, any fitting that held oil cups was called a *lampier*, and a *godet* was a small oil cup with a floating wick. Until the Fifteenth Century *bobèche* meant the candle socket, but during the second half of the century it came to mean the drip pan.

The *flambeaux* was originally a Gothic term for the torch made from a bundle of reeds. Its later use refers to very large candles or pitched rope. The ancestor of the standard lamp was the crown of light on a stem or on tripod feet, sometimes simple but more often ornate, and this was called the *couronne de lumière pédiculées* (Plate 13).

A *chandelier d'appliqué* was a bracket for hanging on the wall and was introduced as a fashionable candle holder during the Fourteenth Century. The *chandelier à huile* was known in England as a peg lamp, and was basically a small oil lamp with floating wick which was fitted into the socket of a candlestick; and the *torsièr* was a wrought iron standard to hold a flaming torch. The *chandelle* was a candle. Candlesticks were in abundance, more especially after the Renaissance, and were made with or without drip pans. Their names are of interest to the student, and a few are noted here for guidance:

bougie a small household candle set on the pricket or in the socket of a *bougeoir*, a small, shallow candlestick which was

13 Couronne de lumière pédiculées, *Fifteenth Century.*

also known as *pallete, cresset* or *esconce.*

chandelier à bobèche a candlestick with a socket.

chandelier à bortrole a candlestick with a socket which had an opening for removal of the candle.

chandelier à fleurs a candlestick with floral patterns in coloured enamel or gilt.

chandelier à lobes a candlestick of pottery, enamel or metal, made in the form of a bundle of reeds.

chandelier à personnage in bronze, silver or wood, a life-size or half-life-size figure of a servant holding a candelabra.

chandelier à point a candlestick with a pricket.

chandelier bassets a low candle holder with pricket set directly on the base. Displaced in the Fourteenth Century by the foot, stem and socket type.

chandelier de voyage a candlestick with two or three detachable components for travelling.

chandelier palmatoir a hand candlestick.

As the impact of the early Renaissance matured under the patronage of Francis I (1515–47), the era distinguished itself by the mingling of French-Gothic and Italian Renaissance influences, thereby creating a time of transition from the old to the new – the new which was to emerge with eternal greatness through the Kings Louis of France. Lighting fittings became less ponderous in the hands of the newly inspired designers, who used shapes and decoration with varying degree of skill and understanding.

An early Renaissance candlestick stands on three scrolled feet with the stem in hexagonal urn shaped segments separated by turned discs and surmounted by a turreted drip pan bearing a pricket (Plate 14). This would have been made in either bronze, brass or wood. Eventually everything became heavily ornamented with Renaissance designs. The Sixteenth Century *chandelier* (table candlestick) was in bronze, the base being similar to an inverted, short-stemmed cup supported on scrolled legs. The stem was surrounded with whimsies

14 Renaissance chandelier, *Fifteenth Century.*

silvered, or polychromed in red, green and blue.

Especially rare pieces of the Sixteenth Century are the candlesticks of glazed and coloured pottery made between 1530 and 1560 near Oiron, and therefore called Oiron ware. Since the production of these beautiful candlesticks was most notable during the reign of Henry II (1549–59) they are also called *Henri Deux* candlesticks.

Made of fine white clay, their hand-painted arabesques, initials and lacy patterns, were immersed beneath a thin lemon colour transparent glaze. The designs are in bold relief and include devices such as wreaths, shells and human figures; for the student of ceramics these pieces reward detailed inspection.

Fine chandeliers were commissioned by the ruling classes who were able to engage the services of the most skilled workmen, and those fittings became the treasures of the land and the pride of their owners. The Parisian silversmith, Guilliume Herondelle, was favoured by the court of Francis I, and in 1538 made a silver hanging chandelier on instructions from the king himself. But wrought iron was probably more extensively used than any other material, and the wall brackets of the Henry II period are particularly noted for their style and vigour.

One such model is mounted on a vertical backplate scrolled top and bottom. A straight square-section arm projects forward to hold the scroll-covered post which bears the grease pan. The edge of the pan is decorated by a deep rim with scalloped and *fleur-de-lis* motifs and the candle is held in a simple socket. Between the post and the backplate is a large

or grotesques, and was topped by a deep candle cup. Candlesticks of large proportions found place in home and church alike, and many were made in the style of the Netherlands chandeliers which now enjoyed widespread popularity throughout almost all of Europe.

Carved wood fittings, both hanging and free-standing, were in walnut, often reversed C-scroll with a floral motif at its centre (Plate 15). A more delicate version of this theme is to be seen in a bracket which projects forward and upwards on two C-scrolls overlaid with leaf work, and the deep pan has tassels hanging from the scallops, an influence as Spanish as the C-scrolls are Italian in their application.

Candle light was destined to reign supreme for another three hundred or so years, but a good deal of attention was being devoted to developing a more effective method of lighting by increasing the efficiency of oil lamps; a task that produced many incidental variations on basic ideas but was limited in its potentials by the absence of a suitable fluid for burning.

In trying to appreciate the difficulties of making a really efficient lamp, we must bear in mind that the thin by-product of petroleum known as paraffin was not discovered in quantity until about 1856, although mineral oil from Burma was in limited supply well before then, and camphene was not used until the early 1800s. Lamp oils such as colza oil, olive oil and whale oil, were expensive and not easy to obtain, and lard-burning lamps – which required a special burner – were not introduced until about 1840.

It was, therefore, of some moment, when in 1550, Jerome Cardan, an Italian doctor of medicine, invented a lamp with a fountain feed system which kept the wick steadily supplied with oil from a font set above the wick support so that the lamp continued to burn evenly and for long periods without attention.

In size, the lamp was quite small being only five or six inches in height, and while many were produced during the next two hundred years, they were not available to the poorer classes who made do with their long familiar oil pans and clay lamps. Even so, Cardan's lamp neither gave more light nor improvement in distribution, since, like all other lamps, when it was hanging on the wall it cast a dark shadow below, and there was still no method of increasing the brightness of the flame.

Meanwhile, in Italy and Spain, the poor burned their smelly, smokey oils and fats, and the French and Far Eastern rulers introduced an element of elegance by

15 Bras de lumière, c.1550.

burning exotic perfumes, which gave off more fragrance than illumination.

By the time of Cardan's lamp, the most popular chandeliers of the day came from the Netherlands, and were made to special order according to the requirements of the purchaser. The central shaft was of solid brass or bronze, in baluster form of vase and sphere shapes separated by turned members. The arms formed graceful S-scrolls radiating in one or more tiers from the shaft which terminated in a large solid ball.

It was common practice to fit a large ring to the end of the lower sphere so that a smaller chandelier could be hung there if additional light was needed. In the loftier residence the fittings were suspended on decorated cord and tassel suspensions, a device which the old Moors had introduced into Spain during the glorious days of their domination.

LOUIS XIII
By the time Louis XIII (reigned 1610–43) ascended the throne at the age of nine years, France had begun to attract world attention with her own original designs and with the grand period which we usually class as the Baroque. At that time, the Huguenots were skilled craftsmen and talented designers in silver and gold, and many beautiful candelabra and chandeliers originated from their hands; but their open disagreement over the young king's marriage to a Spanish princess found disfavour in the eyes of the ruthless Cardinal Richelieu, and in the events which followed their persecution, the majority of the Huguenots fled to England or to the Netherlands, where their skills were readily employed to advantage.

The significance of this unhappy episode is that it marks a decisive period for the introduction of French influence abroad and provides a starting point from which to recognise the mingling of French styles with designs elsewhere.

Towards the end of the reign we find a few changes in the terms being used for lighting fittings. Candlesticks were no longer called *chandeliers*, but *flambeaux*. Hanging lights were called *candélabres*. Wall brackets with mirror back-plates reflecting the candle light now came into limited use and were known as *plaques en miroir*. A typical wall bracket of the Louis XIII period was in the form of a human hand emerging from a circular or oval backplate and grasping the fluted shaft of a flaming torch. This would be carved from oak or walnut and naturalistically coloured.

Chandeliers (now called *candélabres*) generously hung with cut glass pendants in a variety of shapes had originated in Italy, but before the half-century had turned, several French-inspired designs were introduced, some from the glassworks at Bacarrat.

The semi-precious rock crystal pendants, cut and polished by hand, projected a fantasy of prismatic colours, shimmering and scintillating by day and darting pin-points of brilliant light between the flickering candles by night.

In contrast, for the less opulent surrounds and for the less wealthy citizens, the torch was a cheaper and more convenient device, as it could be demounted and taken about as needed, and since the making of fine chandeliers was in the hands of only a few skilled workers, something less exalted would be produced by the blacksmith or the armourer for general-purpose lighting.

One widely used table candlestick of the period consisted of a candle socket mounted directly onto a wide drip pan which stood on three bowed feet, rather like cabriole legs. A rod rising from the outer edge of the pan had attached to it an adjustable backplate as the reflector. The most terminated at the top with the *fleur de lis* motif.

The reign of Louis XIII was contemporary with those of James I and Charles I in England. It is noted for the merging of Italian Renaissance ornament with the Flemish, for the superb handling of foliage, figures and masks, for the introduction of the grand Baroque style of architecture and furnishings; for the new importance of the oil lamp, and for the developing of cultural elements which made France an originator of style and fashion in her own right.

LOUIS XIV

As Louis XIV (reigned 1643–1715) was an infant at the time of his accession, and the country was governed by his mother, Anne of Austria, until 1660 – a regency that was ably supported by the powerful Cardinal Mazarin whose name enjoys immortality in lighting history as well as in statesmanship.

In 1642, the Italo-French cardinal, statesman, Jules Mazarin (1602–61) succeeded to the position of First Minister on the death of Richeleau, an appointment which ensured the advantages necessary for him to pursue the arts in which he delighted. A designer of furnishings and

16 *Mazarin chandelier, c.1650.*

architecture, he had no difficulty in turning his attention to the shaping and decoration of lighting fittings for the glorification of state apartments, and in this connection he is noted for the magnificent hanging chandeliers in which he freely used decorative motifs in the form of women's heads, bearded men on formal scroll work and theatrical masks intermingled with leafwork (Plate 16).

The Mazarin chandeliers, in gold or silver or bronze, became works of art to be imitated abroad with as much care and attention to detail as befitted the finer craftsmen. The English version of these chandeliers is notable not only for its reproduction of the essential features but also for its restraint in avoiding over-elaboration.

The reign is distinctive for having introduced good taste and beauty into furnishing and architecture to the entire continent, and is, in particular, regarded as the great period of French lighting.

Crystal *candélabres* and *giranole* became extremely elaborate, and although the difference between the terms in obscure it is likely that the *candélabres* is the larger and more elaborate of the two.

As terms changed once again, the hanging chandeliers became known as *lustres,* and those typical of the period were made in brass or *bronze doré* heavily draped with rock crystal pendants of different designs. The framework was shaped either like a large vase or a jar in the earlier models, and was lyre-shaped towards the latter years of the period. These frames rose upwards from the base and curved outwards at the top, every movement of the design intending to show off the hand-cut pendants which depended from it.

Pendants came in several sizes and in different shapes, each with its own particular design and decorative cut. Tall crystal spires rose amid the visual tinkle of the pendants, and a large crystal sphere hung from the base of the shaft as an artistic finial.

The *lustre à lacé* had its metal framework entirely overlaid with glass borders, intertupted at the joins by glass marguerites, and it was profusely dressed with interlacing garlands and leaf-like pendeloques. In the *lustre à tige découverte* the stem was composed of spheres, urns and knops, and the arms, which commenced at the candles cups, curved back and upwards in the lyre-shaped outline which distinguishes the later period. Everywhere about the framework is seen tall spires, pendants and festoons of beads, reflecting the light and breaking into rainbow colours the light that passed through them.

Chandeliers appliqué, wall brackets, were made in matching designs and were made to accommodate a large number of candles.

The most notable of the beautiful *lustres à cristaux* were installed in the Palace at Versailles to become world-famous as state treasures and to be regarded as the templates for reproduction pieces right down to our own times.

Lighting fittings made of crystal, *bronze doré, ormolu* and silver, were designed by the elite of French artists, and many chandeliers, after the style of Mazarin, were overlaid with acanthus leaf and scrollwork, and made more elaborate with masks, satyrs and human figures.

It was Charles Andre Boulle (1642–1732), the royal chief cabinet maker, who popularised the use of the ormolu process to make applied decorations for furniture, and similar ornamentation was employed as decorative features on chandeliers and candelabra, not only by him but by other great designers such as Stella, Blondel, Vinet, Ballin and Bérain.

As glass-making techniques improved it became possible to imitate fine rock crystal by melting a refined glass formula which the Bohemians called 'crystal glass', and, except in those cases where only the best would suffice, the new crystal developed as a beautiful and less expensive substitute for the semi-precious rock crystal, especially as it was now possible to make a clearly transparent glass.

From as early as 1670 horse caravans from Bohemia travelled through Poland and the Baltic States, Denmark, Holland, Germany and France, bringing their beautiful glassware to the principal merchants in the cities, wresting the world glass trade from the Venetians, who had long enjoyed unchallenged superiority.

By 1657 many fashionable residences boasted a crystal chandelier, but it was not until the last thirty years of the century that this privilege could be called widespread, and little is known about the development of lighting fittings in those old glass works.

The making of glass was largely in the hands of part-time craftsmen who had inherited their secrets from previous generations of glassmakers. Technical conditions were inadequate, factories were situated well off the main travel routes, and there were no regular working hours. During the periods when the factories were idle the workers followed other occupations, waiting while the raw materials were collected, sorted and prepared for melting.

The point at which the molten glass was judged to be in a workable condition was reached at any time during the day or night, and the workers were then warned to attend the factory.

Immediately they left their homes for the factories where they commenced a twelve- to fourteen-hour shift, working until all the glass had been made up according to the orders which had been obtained while the materials were being assembled and selected.

The caravans often carried chandelier glass made to special order for the Court or wealthy citizens, and by the 1700s there was as much Bohemian glass as there was French in the light fittings of Paris and other principal cities.

Apart from crystal chandeliers and silver candlesticks there were beautiful pole lanterns which were used along corridors and in large salons, and even out of doors as the forerunner of the street lantern. One such lantern of about 1700 was a tapering, six-sided candle lantern with scrollwork on top and windows of opaque glass. The lantern was mounted on a thick pole which was covered in velvet and had a carved wood decoration in gilt, the whole standing on a base supported on four feet.

In architecture, the Baroque had passed its fashionable popularity and its aggressive, theatrical presence lost favour with new designers. The formal, defined curved outlines of the earlier Baroque styles were now overlaid with leaf ornament to break up the severity of the design.

An encouraging figurehead in this change of inspiration was Jean Baptiste Colbert (1619–1683) a statesman and patron of the arts whom Mazarin had introduced to Louis XIV and whom Louis appointed Controller General of the Finances.

In the applied foliage decoration of the emerging new style, gilded metals played a major role in ormolu and *cuivre doré*. They were formed in delicate acanthus leaf scrolls; appeared more vigorously as oak or ivy leaf, or were draped in lacy garlands. Other common decoration was in the form of trophies of victory, arms, cupids, and horns of plenty (cornucopias).

Antoine Watteau (1684–1721) a famous painter and interior decorator, found considerable favour among the nobility with his interpretation of these motifs, and he exerted a great influence on interior decoration well into the following reign.

The three principal gold finishes were

ormolu, cuivre doré and *bronze doré,* all of which were very costly and required great skill in their application. The *ormolu* process was originally produced in the early Eighteenth Century, and is the process of gilding bronze or brass by amalgamating pure gold with mercury. The article for treatment was covered with the mixture, probably by dipping, and the mercury evaporated by the application of a heat process which left the gold completely adhering to the article.

Cuivre doré is copper gilded with gold leaf, and *bronze doré* is bronze or brass gilded in the same manner.

Brass, an alloy of copper and zinc, and bronze, an alloy of copper, zinc and tin, were produced in solid rather than in the tubular or hollow form, and in its newly made state did not have such a rich colour as gold and was easily tarnished. Most of the great Netherlands chandeliers were in the unpolished metal and needed to be cleaned with oil to prevent rusting. It is understandable, therefore, that the French workmen should wish to avoid this defect by applying a layer of gold leaf when the occasion allowed.

Increased attention was paid to lantern making, and many were most exquisitely carved from linden wood or walnut, being finished in a high natural polish or in rich colours. There were even designs in which candle arms were added to the lantern framework so that the light must be augmented.

The Italian-Flemish influence still lingered on from the Louis XIII styles, and the resplendent Baroque continued to inspire designers for years to come.

The end of the reign was contemporary with that of Queen Anne in England, and was distinguished by the work of two great ministers, Mazarin and Colbert. The most distinctive lighting fittings of the era were those pendant-draped frames of vase or lyre shape which were destined to become even more celebrated during the next reign. Notable also was the previously mentioned introduction of Bohemian 'crystal glass', as a less expensive rival to the natural rock crystal. Finally, there was the beginning of a new style which had yet to mature and was yet to be named.

By gathering around himself the galaxy of artists and men of letters who responded to his royal patronage, the 'Grand Monarque', in no small way contributed to the age which is acknowledged as one of the most glorious in French history, and *Le style Louis Quatorze* will always be distinguished among the scholars of the world.

LOUIS XV

Louis XV (reigned 1715–74) served his minority with Philip Duke of Orleans as Regent, and while the regency periods of his predecessors have remained academically undistinguished the regency of Louis XV has become a distinctive 'period' in its own right and is called *le Régence* (1715–23).

Outstanding among practical cabinet makers of the day was Charles Cressent (1685–1768) whose furniture was veneered and ormolu mounted. He was a gifted wood carver and bronze worker, and became chief cabinet maker of the *Régence* period, being responsible for some of the most outstanding work of the age. He introduced the outward swelling curved surfaces on furniture which the French call *bombé* shape, and he developed the slender cabriole leg for chairs, tables and commodes, points which are of value to the lighting design consultant when matching lighting fittings to the period.

It was during this *Régence* period that the swing from rigid formality to the abandoned asymmetrical became significant under the direction of the noted goldsmith and architect, Meissonier, whose extraordinary artistic expression created *rococo* art.

Whereas the Baroque is a complete and positive rule governing architecture and furnishing styles, the early *rococo* is the application of naturalistic ornament superimposed on the formality of the previous era, and eventually becomes so dominant in the later period as to leave no trace whatever of the framework.

Deeply carved formal scrolls, distinctly visible amid a profusion of leafage, distinguishes all the decorated furniture and lighting fittings of the *Régence*, a style which shows the mingling of the late Baroque and the early *rococo,* and which is therefore the transitional period between the two.

A wall bracket of the period shows the leafy scrolling effect around a central *cartouche,* which has its candle arms overlaid with acanthus. But the candle sockets are formally turned urns, and the pans are milled or rope-edged (Plate 17).

In the *rococo* the formal framework of brackets was draped with either acanthus or oak leaves and acorns. Candle arms, resembling leafy branches spiralled upwards and outwards to embrace the pans and sockets, which were formed of petals.

Candlesticks, retaining their baluster

17 Régence appliqué, *c.1715.*

silhouette, were an arrangement of swirling leafy ornament which merged down and around the circular base, and upwards to form the drip pans (Plate 18). Multi-light fittings had their branches set at different positions in relation to their fellows, and achieved a spring-like appearance of natural growth.

By 1723, when Louis became King in his own right, the *rocaille,* as it was originally called, had become a whole pattern of design: asymmetric and a profusion of delicately carved ornament resembling shells, foliage, rocks and scrolls, ingeniously fused together in one characteristic fantasy of naturalistic beauty. There was no sign of the formal framework on which the *rocaille* had been born.

18   Rococo candlestick, Eighteenth Century.

Designers developed lighting fittings composed entirely of branch-and-leaf forms, twisting, swirling and growing one over another with the vigour of nature in spring. For example, wall brackets were composed of oak leaves and acorns or overlapping acanthus leaves. The candle arms, like branches, sprouted from the main stem, thrusting delicately outwards and upwards supporting the drip pans and sockets, which were made like overlapping leaves or petals (Plate 19). Grotesques and animals were often used as an integral part of the design. In some brackets, the curling leafage forms the entrance to a lair, and there in the centre a griffin is seen, squatting jauntily against the background, a whimsical, likeable little beast.

Few of those brackets were small. Intended only for luxury surroundings they were, therefore, on a grand scale, even four or five feet tall, with fifteen-inch candles held in leafy sockets.

Identified with this period, which we call *le style Louis Quinze,* is the introduction of candle branches fitted to furniture; to mirrors, writing desks, bed-posts, bed-heads, chair arms, door posts, fireplaces and wash stands. Even the tripod fire-screen, with its tapestry picture, became the bearer of one or more candle arms, and before long the screen was removed, the feet fitted with castors and the central shaft adapted to bear several adjustable candle arms, and it emerged with some triumph as the moveable candle stand for use in the drawing room, the music room and the library.

The background which complemented these beautiful fittings was typically and vividly French: a lofty room with coved ceiling, its walls covered in inexpensive tapestries and its high chimney piece rising and merging into the ceiling. Between the high narrow windows, pier mirrors reflected the candlelight from the *girandole* (a branching chandelier) which occupied the elegant tables below them.

19   Rococo appliqué, c.1728

There are no comparisons today by which we can judge the effect of the multiple use of candles on the vast scale used by the predecessors of our heads of state. There is, however, ample evidence to show the extent of the illumination provided on state occasions in old prints, paintings and lithographs. An intricate illustration of the candle-lit funeral of King Philip V of Spain at Notre Dame, Paris, depicts one of those occasions and appears in Plate 20.

The great *lustres à cristaux* of the *Louis Quinze* period were the height of luxury and were both expensive and intricate in their production. The whole chandelier was made and assembled at the glassworks to ensure perfection of shape and fit. It was then disassembled, packed and transported to the site, where specialist workmen, sometimes the makers themselves, set about the task of assembling the frame, suspending it in position and hanging about it the hundreds of pendants and swags which distinguished the style.

The entire framework was composed of lyre-shaped members encased in short lengths of glass, ascending rather like a well-designed tree with candle arms branching off the main stem. A myriad of shimmering pendants hung from the *corona* and descended to the cut glass finial below the shaft (Plate 21).

Other *lustres* had a central shaft composed of ball, urn and vase shapes in cut class which reflected hundreds of star-points of candlelight.

So impressive and coveted were crystal chandeliers that crowned heads and state rulers came from far and near to see them. Many orders were given to the glass factories, but comparatively few lustres

20   *Candle lit funeral of King Philip V of Spain, at Nôtre Dame, Paris*

21 Lustre à cristaux, *Eighteenth Century.*

from Rouen. Every petal, leaf and branch comprising the bracket or hanging fitting was delightfully painted in detail, and every technique was employed to represent the fittings as living forms with flowers and leaves realistically applied to suggest a beautiful flowering branch.

Dinanderie, champlevé, Limoges enamel and Chinese ornament retained their value and place among the treasures of the household. In fact the Chinese influence gained considerable importance among the furnishings and decorations of the aristocracy, and was destined to exercise a profound impact on design in England.

Not all rooms were fitted with *lustres,* the principal lighting was by means of wall lights, *appliques,* or *girandole* for the table, or brackets, *bras de lumière,* which were fitted to furniture as a localised light source.

Down the social scale and into the kitchen or the servants' quarters one might find small candlesticks, the pan lamp or the bronze hand lamp of olden days still in daily use, and the average eighteenth-century family in the surrounding countryside burned rushlights or splints, aided perhaps by grease lamps which burned soft fat feeding a fibre wick. The disadvantage of such lamps was that, before ignition could be accomplished, the fat had to be melted to a manageable consistency and then maintained in that condition to ensure continuous burning. For this reason, in colder climates, the lamp was kept close to the hearth in order to derive some of its warmth from the fire which invariably burned there.

The crusie, an iron pan with a pinched wick support, was ideally suited to most

were made for use in other countries. Glass makers, in particular chandelier makers, were limited in number and consequently enjoyed the patronage of an exclusive clientèle.

Nevertheless some privileges were extended when the power of demand was great enough. For example, Maria Theresia, Empress of Austria from 1740 to 1780, was so enchanted by the crystal chandeliers of Louis's Court that she had similar models made and installed throughout the principal rooms in her palace. This particular style of hanging fitting is now universally known as a 'Maria Theresia' chandelier, and is still made in Czechoslovakia, in the old Bohemian glassworks, for our delight and admiration.

The urge to reproduce naturalistic floral lighting fittings was further perpetuated by some exquisite work in enamelled metal climates since it could be used to burn fat or oil, whichever was more readily obtainable, but generally the lack of a thin oil, such as could be pressed from nuts and olives, was either expensive or not in circulation to the poorer classes.

The tinsmith was probably the most prolific lamp maker of the times, and he would travel the countryside, mostly on foot, with all sorts of lamps and candlesticks hung about his person for all to see. His trade as a purveyor of lamps and lighting fittings was probably as old as the Seventeenth Century and because of the low price of tin and the relative ease with which it was worked, he was no doubt a more successful lighting salesman than were his contemporaries, the blacksmith who worked in iron, the brazier who worked in brass and the coppersmith who made his lamps from copper.

In contrast, on the levels of society which employed the crystal maker, the goldsmith and the silversmith, craftsmen had become so particular that each material in which they worked was accorded a special treatment. Wood was deeply carved and boldly worked to a fine finish, waxed or polychromed. Gold was worked with the greatest possible delicacy and fineness; silver, somewhat more vigorously; bronze with aggressive firmness, and iron with strength and vigour.

Ribbon-bow knots, tassels, scrolls, acanthus, floral swags, urns and *rocaille* ornament, spread from the designs and deft fingers of Oppenordand and Caffiéri, and the sons and pupils of Boulle. Human figures, nymphs, satyrs, griffins, cupids and groups of Pan-like figures playing Pan pipes, were contributed by the goldsmith Meissionier.

The initial effect of the Italian Renaissance was now some two hundred years past. Europe had derived wonderful ideas and ideals from it, and an entirely new mode of living had emerged for those in a position to patronise it. Architecture, art, ornament, fashion, education and social graces had all been affected as fashion dictators moulded mind and matter almost as one, until no one believed that anything of great consequence could again excite the imagination of the civilised world.

The discovery of long-lost ancient Rome had almost faded as an historical event, when, in 1706, there came news from Italy of fresh excavations which had revealed the old cities of Herculaneum and Pompeii, lying entombed in the volcanic ash and dried mud which had cascaded from the erupting Vesuvius in A.D. 79.

The stricken cities gave up their secrets with painful slowness, first because little action was taken after the initial discovery, and secondly because both finance and labour were not easily come by; but little by little the surface soil was dug away to find what lay beneath. The results were astonishing.

Statues, statuettes, jewellery, mosaics, furniture, decorations, murals and utensils were delicately extracted from the earth as excited excavators eventually came to grips with the task. Architectural designs and principles of construction, hitherto associated only with the later Byzantine and Roman architects, came to the light of day.

Among the treasures were found beautiful hanging lamps with three-, four- or five-wick spouts mounted around a central font and suspended on chains or ropes, and these at once provided a popular pattern for fresh designs. Hand lamps in bronze and terracotta, some mounted with human figures, were eagerly examined and catalogued among the other amazing links with the past. By the 1740s fresh interest had been aroused in the style of classical furniture and interior decoration, an interest which was especially keen amongst those ladies who commanded the most influential positions at Court.

Strange to relate, the acceptance of the fashions which mark the great period of French history from Louis XV to Louis XVI, was almost entirely at the whim of two notorious yet not unsuccessful women – Pompadour and Du Barry. The Marquise de Pompadour (1721–64) had influenced the affairs of the kingdom for twenty years. A woman of taste and intelligence, a patroness of the arts and lover of culture, she was largely responsible for the King's acceptance of the *rococo* and its attendant ornamentation. In 1748 she sent a mission of archaeologists to Pompeii to study and to report on the discoveries in the fullest possible manner. It was their research which lead directly to the Classical Revival, which although commenced under *Louis Quinze*, reached its zenith in the succeeding reign.

The Countess Du Barry (1746–93) enjoyed wealth, power and influence, especially after the death of Pompadour in 1764, and exercised considerable influence on fashionable thinking and trends in furnishing. Undeniably unpopular, she nonetheless enjoyed the obvious intimate attentions of the King. Conscious of her unaristocratic background, she endeavoured to make amends by patronising artists, chandelier makers and fashionable designers.

Candlelight was still predominently the accepted light source; oil lamps had barely progressed beyond the wick-in-oil principle, and Cardan's lamp was probably still the pattern for most of the better class of oil burning device. In all, the amount of light was small, but in 1773, Leger, recognising the potential of an efficient lamp, introduced a flat wick of woven cotton which increased the area of illumination.

The most usual attempts at making oil lamps were confined to pouring oil into a glass container and using a wick threaded through a cork float, making what is now known as a 'drop burner'. In later modifications the float was provided with a short tube that held the wick in a vertical position. It seems that most of these vertical burners were used with peg lamps, a spherical glass font open at the top for the oil and wick and moulded to a peg at the bottom so that they could be fitted into candle sockets or bottle tops (Plate 22).

It was a long reign. In England, George I, George II, and George III had each actively disliked the French, but had found no hesitation in admiring their manners and acquisitions.

The reign is distinguished first by the Régence and the transition from Baroque to Rococo; secondly by the development of crystal chandeliers and the special designs which identify them, thirdly by the serpentine or bow front on furniture, the introduction of the cabriole leg, marquetry and ormolu mounts, and finally by the full extravagance of the Rococo, which to

Louis XVI, married to Marie Antoinette since 1770, came to the throne in 1774. He optimistically set himself the task of restoring the ruined finances, but failure to do this brought not only widespread discontent, but also the Revolution and the guillotine.

At the beginning of the reign, the Rococo, which had inspired the Court of his grandfather, was a discarded fashion. A new generation of talented architects and designers had already established the Classic Revival under the leadership of the older masters. Boulle had tutored Oeben; Oeben had tutored his son Phillippe and also Riesener, who now became chief cabinet maker to Louis.

Furniture in white and gilt had, towards the 1760s, captured the attention of those seeking a change from the general style of 'prestige' furnishings, and ideas were afoot to banish the cabriole leg in favour of the straight, fluted tapering leg which distinguishes the furniture of the period. Serpentine and bow fronts gave way to straight edges, and a preponderance of ormolu mounts and marquetry abound in the decorative devices distinguishing the style.

Chandeliers, candelabra, candlesticks, *appliques* and *girandoles* were now made with the modifications which had been slowly integrated with other furnishing styles during the transitional period between 1755 and 1770, so that by 1774 the new trends were already in being.

The period of transition shows how the exclusive use of acanthus and oak leaf was discontinued in favour of restricting it to overlaying the candle branches or encasing the lower limbs of human figures.

22   *Glass peg lamp, Eighteenth Century.*

experts everywhere will always be recognised as *le style Louis Quinze*.

LOUIS XVI
None of the previous monarchs had escaped his share of war or revolution, but the grandson and successor of Louis XV was to experience the most disastrous personal failure of the century.

We may see, for example, a wall bracket with the backplate composed of a tapering column surmounted by an urn. The candle branches spring from either side of the column in shallow 'C' curves overlaid by leafwork. The candles are held in decorative urn-like cups. A similar bracket had its candle arms emerging from a spray of leafwork surmounted by a large bow. The candle cups were fluted and the edges of the drip pans were made like circles of thick rope.

On another the half figure of a woman was used as the backplate, the lower limbs disappearing into clinging leafwork. Her outstretched arms merged into the leaves which overlayed the C-scroll branches, and the drip pans were delicately curling leaves and petals.

Meissionier's 'Piping Boy', a charming little cherub blowing into twin pipes, was introduced as the backplate for a wall bracket with 'C'-scroll branches, and its subsequent development was to provide one of the characteristic designs of the period.

As the transitional period drew to a close, the pure forms of the new designs stood alone on their own merit, and it was possible to note that the basic style was derived from straight lines – formal, graceful, distinctive and elegant, and that certain motifs were the decorative features adopted by the leading masters.

Ormolu mounts were beautifully chiselled animal heads, laurels, acanthus, nude figures, masks, bows and tassels. Porcelain plaques from Sèvres and Dresden were inserted into door and cabinet panels, and were used inset in oval or round frames on wall brackets.

The favourite material used for lighting fittings was *bronze doré, cuivre doré, argenté, brun* and *vert antique;* silver being the popular material for the dining table, gold for the salon or drawing rooms, bronze for the library and the hall.

Three distinct methods of decoration emerged from all the efforts to beautify the furnishings of the period. First there was the neo-Classic with its use of Classic forms such as goats' heads, reeding, fluting, gadrooning and cupids mingling with leafwork and garlands. Second there was the exquisite use of rustic work, with leaves and petals and porcelain figures. Third was the introduction of Chinese porcelains and the pretty use of pagodas and figures amid the rustic pastoral scenes in *le mode chinoise.* Chandelier arms, or branches as they were often called, had lost the S-scroll form of the previous designs and now followed the shape of a 'C' lying on its back; that end which attached to the centre shaft of the fitting curled upwards and inwards while the outer end curved upwards to hold the pans and sockets for the candles. The metalwork was overlaid with lengths of acanthus, gently curling at the tips. In some models, an independent scroll was included slightly above but following the line of the candle arm, and this continued to turn inwards on itself until it terminated in a leaf-tip or flower-head. In some models, the S-scroll arm was used attached to a tall backplate, ornamented by masks and leaves and surmounted by a long tibbon and bow. The arms were overlaid with leafwork and have attendant scrolls springing around the scroll. Such a model was designed by Delafosse and the work

23 *Ribbon-bow* appliqué, *c.1755*.

and not without a touch of humour. Since 1349 the heir presumptive to the French throne had always been called the *Dauphin*, and so the use of the creature as a decorative motif was a good-humoured play on words, and he appeared in many roles. Now with his curling tail as the handle on an exquisite gold candlestick; then in a group of three, forming the base of a candlestick with tails held aloft to support the pan and socket. Here, seen curling whimsically down the stem of a candelabra. There, to decorate the powder bowl in my lady's boudoir.

Leaders of the developing styles were the architects, Percier and Fontaine, who designed architecture, decoration and furnishing to conform to a master plan. Fontaine supplied the architectural skill while Percier attended to the interior decoration. Two of the most brilliant craftsmen of the age were the bronze workers, Gouthiére and Thomire, the former made cupids and female figures, the latter specialised in classic Roman styles; and these gentlemen were largely responsible for executing Perciers' designs in bronze, *bronze doré* and silver.

Falconet, the noted sculptor, designed nymphs standing on pedestals and holding aloft sprays of flowers in which the blossoms conceal the candle cups. The figures were in *bronze brun* or patinated, that is to say, finished so as to represent the dark green coating acquired by antique bronze, and they were mounted on a short round column attached to a square flat base of dark marble, the division between the two materials being concealed by a band of gold. Similar pieces by Boizot are equally as attractive and continue to demonstrate

executed by the *ciseleur* Pagot in ormolu (Plate 23).

The rustic influence was to be seen in a delicately made *appliqué* with upward curving branches, covered with leaves and ending in entwined petals for the candle cups, the whole being attached to a tall ribbon and bow backplate which terminated in a tassel.

There was also the charming use of the dolphin, a popular and likeable sea creature whose physical design appealed to the creative genius of the furniture makers, the popularity of the use of nymphs and flowers.

Large golden chandeliers used as the central device on the shaft, a group of cherubs playing Pan pipes, their lower limbs disappearing into the overlaid acanthus work of the slender C-scroll arms and their curly heads bowed in concentration as they blow steadily into their golden pipes. Matching wall brackets repeat every characteristic of the chandelier, and represent an elegant suite of fittings which are characteristic of the middle period (Plate 24).

The cornucopia, or trumpet-shaped socket, preceded fittings in which the candle arms were composed of circular hunting horns, with the bell of the horn concealing the candle cup. With this type of design fittings began to be made without the large incurving scroll and the majority of their leaf overlay. Fresh ideas for design and décor were being introduced as the end of the century came in sight, although many of the existing patterns were destined to continue, modified perhaps, but nonetheless distinctively Louis Seize.

For example, the convex mirror, set in a circular gilded frame with little golden spheres contained between the inner and outer edges, is known as the Antoinette mirror, but in the succeeding Empire period an eagle was added to it.

The *chandelier à abat-jour*, a shaded candlestick, was one of the most significant pieces of the period. Basically it was a sturdy, fluted or baluster column, mounted on either a three-stepped circular base or a square plinth with lions' paws, and having two or more candle arms about two-thirds of the way up the stem. The central shaft

24 *Piping boy* appliqué, Eighteenth Century.

was terminated at the top by an ornamental handle and supported a circular iron shade with slightly sloping sides. It is significant because it represents the ancestor of the modern shaded table lamp and was destined to become a symbol of forthcoming Empire styles.

Of even greater importance, technologically, was the new development in the efficiency of the oil lamp, still a preoccupation with established as well as would-be inventors. Aimé Argand (1755–1803), a Swiss chemist and physician, who was working in France from 1782 to 1784, improved upon Leger's arrangement of a flat wick by making a much wider wick and forming it into a cylinder around a central tube. This was fitted into the opening at the top of the lamp font so that the lower end of the wick trailed in the oil. The cylinder allowed air to pass through to the burning end of the wick, thereby increasing the rate of burning and consequently affecting the amount of light.

In order to achieve a perfectly steady flame a glass cylinder or chimney was added to protect the wick and to increase the flow of air. For the first time a new future for the oil-burning lamp could be visualised, but even now, the whole problem had not been solved. Although the system could produce twelve times the amount of light than had hitherto been possible, the use of the heavy colza oil* did not allow for a simple wick-in-oil system such as was possible in less efficient types of lamp. It was necessary to place the main oil font at a higher level than the chamber which fed the wick so that the heavy oil was gravity-fed to the burner, an arrangement which later became familiar in the popularly named 'Student Lamp'.

In the meantime it was the candle lantern that continued to attract the attentions of designers and craftsmen, and often their enthusiasm for elaboration produced artistic masterpieces which, for reasons of cost alone, would never be reproduced in modern times. Every decorative device of the period went into these wonderful lanterns of *bronze doré;* there were trophies, cupids, trumpets, cherubs, bells, flaming torches and quivers filled with arrows, all carefully arranged amid wreaths, foliage, scrolls and drapes.

These lanterns were based on the typical Louis XVI chandelier with eight or ten scrolled branches supporting cupids and leafwork as part of the central shaft. A large cylindrical framework of *bronze doré* and crystal glass surrounded the candle branches, and this was elaborately ornamented with leafwork, flower heads and ribbon bows. The scrolled supports of the *corona* of the lantern were rich in applied motifs, such as wreaths, horns, drapes and golden cord, all most beautifully worked in metal by the finest *ciseleur* of the era.

The cylindrical lanterns for indoor use on stairways, and in entrance halls and salons were as elaborate as they could be made, and there was apparently no limit to the ingenuity of the craftsmen who endeavoured, and succeeded, in translating their ideas into solid forms. Cylindrical lanterns for external use were made for carriages and coaches, and had a candle post attached to the base which also served to hold the lantern in a ring-socket attached to the coachwork. The top of the lantern finished in a two- or three-tier smoke-bell, and this was often surmounted by a brass or bronze finial in the shape of a flaming torch. Most of these coach lanterns were made of cast iron, some were of brass and some were of tin, and all were destined to play their part in history, their individual beauty for long afterwards an inspiration to those of educated taste.

In contrast, as we return to the lower strata of living, we find a vastly different set of standards. Lacemaking happened to be one of the crafts by which some women and children were still able to make a meagre living. As they worked, closely and industriously, in cramped, unhygienic conditions, their skilful creations were barely

---

*Colza oil was produced from rape seed (*Brassica Napus*, a plant related to the cabbage). It was also used as a lubricant, and in the manufacture of soap.

illuminated by a light source which, on its introduction in 1613, had been described by John Rovenzon as 'a new devised luminary of glass'.

This consisted of a table top mounted on a rough stand. A tallow candle, held in a socket or a small candlestick in the centre of the table, shed its single light into flasks of water mounted in wooden holders around the circumference of the table top.

The flasks enlarged the area of light and threw a concentrated patch of brightness on to the work being done by nearby lacemakers. Although this type of lamp was also used by block-makers, engravers and jewellers, it is usually regarded as the 'Lacemakers' Condenser'.

The simple ancient night lamp – *le veilleuse,* was still in general use, as was the even more ancient *candil.* The *chandelier à verges,* was a pricket mounted on an iron rod, and the small hand candlestick, the *bougeoir,* was usually in tin, brass or pewter.

A candle wedged into a bottle neck would be more usual in the coffee shops, taverns and poor houses, while brass wick-spout lamps from Belgium sufficed for most of the wealthier merchants.

In the streets, torches and rush lights flickered beside the Sedan chairs, and the horn lantern wavered in the hand of the night watch. The iron pan lamp probably provided the light by which many a revolutionary meeting was conducted, for revolution was close at hand.

Paris was starving. The people were desperate, rough and resentful. Public services, such as they were, did little to assist the needy or to administer the rights of the citizen. Authority largely corrupt, and aggressive above all, administered harsh punishment for petty crimes and found difficulty in maintaining law and order.

Many people were out of work, and even the workers had few home comforts. Their furniture had been handed down from previous generations – carpenter-made benches, stools and tables comprised the family possessions – and for those with no homes there was an uneasy life in the poor-house or a constant wearisome tramp around the streets and markets.

Although the aristocracy continued to indulge itself in fine furnishings, extravagant whims and grand manners, the king found the country's financial problems insoluable. His ministers became impatient and critical; his subjects aggressive and rebellious, and in July 1789 the storming of the Bastille signified the first event in the Revolution. There followed the attempts of the Legislative Council, the attempted escape of Louis and his imprisonment in the Temple until his execution in January 1793.

The reign was contemporary with the early part of George III's in England. It is noted for the change from Rococo to Classic Revival, the new designs in furniture, the invention of the Argand lamp and the introduction of features which were to become famous in the next era, forming the transitional period which precedes the 'pure' elements of each decorative style.

At this point we must take our leave of Louis XVI and the period we know as *le style Louis Seize.*

DIRECTOIRE

A complexity of administrative powers

governed France in its departure from the monarchy, and eventually established two distinctive events which have conveniently served historians and art collectors ever since. Namely, the formation, in October 1795, of the committee known as the Directory of Five, and Napoleon Bonaparte's coup d'etat of November 1799 which overthrew the Directory and established the Consulate (1799–1804) with himself as First Consul.

This was followed in 1804 by events in which Bonaparte had himself invested with Imperial dignity and in so doing brought the French Empire (1804–15) into being.

These are the circumstances of the periods which we call the Directory and the Empire, and which in terms of decoration span the years 1790 to 1815.

The first objects of the Directory were to disparage the way of life established by the monarchy, but while all the trade guilds were dissolved, the most noted craftsmen of the late Louis period were now called upon to design a new foundation for the *régime* of the new Emperor. Percier and Fontaine, Gouthière and Thomire, Riessner and Roentgen, and the cabinet maker George Jacob, were the leaders of this new inspiration, and as these men had already visualised the forms of changing fashion during the last decade of Louis XVI's reign, and their principles had only to be interpreted to suit the pretensions of the new Court.

But while the classic inspiration was revealed in the designs of the Directoire, they were not merely copies of the ancient originals. A good deal of the elaboration of the previous reign was done away with in favour of a more distinctive outline. They retained the modified use of leafwork, reduced the size of the incurving scrollwork on candle branches, retained slender proportions on the branches and emphasised the cornucopia-shaped C-scroll design. They increased the use of the honeysuckle ornament and retained cupids and Roman figures.

An *applique* of the Directoire period is one in which the oval backplate is formed of acanthus leaves from which a delicately cast serpent coils its way left and right supporting three candlesockets formed of overlapping rose petals. The backplate is in *bronze doré* and the serpent in *vert antique*.

Another bracket has a backplate formed of the honeysuckle ornament, one section rising from the centre of the plate, the other projecting from below. Two dolphins with curling tails hold the C-scroll branches in their jaws and the candle cups stand in wide drip pans (Plate 25).

25   Directoire appliqué, *1796–99.*

A Directoire *lustre* is seen to be based on a chain-suspended sanctuary lamp, with a group of cherubs standing in the centre and blowing into raised trumpets. Long, shallow C-scrolls radiate from the circumference of the central bowl and are decorated with leaf tips and flower heads.

Human and mythological figures upheld candlesticks or candle sockets, and the draped or semi-nude figure in *bronze doré*, holding aloft sprays of flowers or a cornucopia, was a typical decoration for the mantle. A popular ornament was a classic urn of porphyry mounted in ormolu with a pair of rams heads at the neck to support sprays of flowers, it was made in pairs and in various sizes according to demand.

Falconet, the sculptor, designed and carved beautiful nymphs in bronze, and he had them standing on a round column of marble, holding a floral array in which candles were contained amid the flowers (Plate 26). The tripod stand of animals' hoofs, griffins, eagles or female torsos, supported elaborate candelabra.

At this time, a *flambeau* was a table lamp with two or three lights; a *candélabre* was a larger model with three or four lights, and the girandole was larger still with four or more lights. The *bobèche* was the drip pan, and the *bobèchon* was a candle socket.

With the mounting successes of Napoleon and the emphasis on military power, the designers turned to motifs like the thunderbolt, the sabre, arrows, wings, torches, laurel and bay wreaths; Phrygian helmets, serpents, lions, eagles' claws, bears' claws, eagles, plumed helmets and stacked flags.

The Egyptian campaign recalled the use of the sphinx, the lotus, palm leaf, and

26 *Clock and candelabrum, Late Eighteenth Century.*

spear which had previously been in use under the monarchy. These were now recreated and made twice as large to complement the occasion, and were augmented by the Egyptian head, the Indian head, the bearded Bacchus, the lyre, the winged horse and the winged lion. Further decoration consisted of the pineapple, acorn, acanthus, honeysuckle or anthemion, the Greek key pattern, rosettes and petals, all of which are well known motifs of the period, and which carry on into the Empire.

The decor and furnishings produced during the four years of the Directoire, are known as *le style Directoire*, and are regarded as the transitional style from Louis XVI to Empire.

As yet there was little interest in ideas for developing the oil lamp. Argand's system remained the best so far, but as each lamp had to be individually made, a good deal of patience was required of a prospective purchaser, and the product still raised an element of suspicion concerning its safety. Even so, some progress was eventually made and there were glass or decorated porcelain oil fonts available with the Argand burner fitted, but the problem of feeding the heavy oil to the wick still occupied the thoughts of lamp makers.

The gravity-feed oil font was replaced in some models by a clockwork driven pump which forced the oil up to the wick for burning. The burning-oil was obtained from the crushed seeds of kale or brassica and was known as carcel or rape-seed oil, or colza oil, either kind being convenient to store and reasonably safe to use. The Carcel lamps with the clockwork pump date from about 1789 and were still being produced one hundred years later.

A popular *applique* which had retained its character from the Louis period was based on the use of hunting horns, so mounted on a long ribbon and tassel backplate that the horns faced upwards like large drip pans, and the candle sockets were concealed within. These horns followed through into the Empire period and became significant among the designs of that period.

EMPIRE

The first nights of the Empire (1804–15) were no doubt made brighter by the multi-candle table *candélabre* which has since become a symbol of the Empire period. The *candélabre* was supported on a decorated baluster stem resting on a square base with four paws, and was comprised of several cornucopia-shaped candle branches encircled above by a large flared iron shade.

A hanging fitting in similar style had its candle holders supported on feathered arrows which radiated from the central shaft as if on their way to some distant target (Plate 27). The shades were decorated with popular motifs and were coloured

27 *Empire* lustre, *c.1804.*

in dark green, red or black, and as black presented a smart contrast with the gold and silver of the period, it was used on many Empire fittings, sometimes as a narrow black band around a crystal chandelier, sometimes to colour a human figure on a candlestick.

The Antoinette convex, circular mirror, was given a black band around the mirror beading leaving the circle of spheres in gold; alternatively the band remained in gold and the spheres were blackened. Often the mirror would be topped by an ebony eagle, wings aspread over deeply carved acanthus scrolls. Scrolled candle branches, hung with crystals, were fitted to either side of the mirror frame.

Empire *candélabres* would show a finely chiselled Roman figure mounted on a cylindrical or hexagonal marble column and holding in the hand a multi-branch candelabra with candle sockets shaped from cornucopia. The Egyptian influence would be shown in either a male or female figure standing on a circular column set into a rim of lotus leaves and resting on a square base of marble. In this, one recognises the upper part of an Egyptian pillar, now inverted so that the column stands vertically above the capital. The figure supported a fluted standard, topped by a wide *bobèche* with scolloped edges, and the candle socket was an urn with a curving lip.

The typical Empire *lustre* was superbly made in *bronze doré*; the body being composed of a shallow basin with a pineapple-shaped finial below and possibly a cupid or flaming crest as the central motif on top; the whole being suspended on decorated link chain from a spray of

28   *Empire* lustre, *c.1809.*

acanthus or palm leaves. The candle branches, from four to twenty-four or more, were of cornucopia C-shape form and were attached to the rim of the body with a small incurving scroll at the base of each arm. The sides and base of the main body were decorated with finely chiselled rams' heads, scrolled cresting and laurel wreaths (Plate 28). In this design we continue to note the resemblance to the early suspended sanctuary lamps.

Furniture was made in mahogany, often stained a vivid red, and was combined with ormolu mounts and upholstery in costly silks. Other woods in common use were tulip, rosewood, satinwood, ebony and beech, all of which were used to fashion chandeliers and wall brackets during this period. It was not uncommon for the more elaborate residence to boast a withdrawing room fitted with a striped silken canopy, its apex gathered at the centre of the ceiling, its drapes falling away to the walls so that the overall effect was that of a large tent such as was used by high ranking officers on the battlefield.

Chairs were elegant with scrolled arms and sabre-shaped legs, the arms sometimes supported on a winged female sphinx or a lion; but not only the furnishings and decor had to be formally classic. Garments also had to come into line with the pretentions of the glory-seeking Empire. Ladies of fashion dressed their hair in the high Grecian style, and wore loose flowing robes to support the illusion.

Napoleon's private apartments in the old palace of the *Tuileries* were furnished after the classic styles of the Egyptian vogue and almost everywhere could be seen marble busts of the Emperor wearing the laurel wreath crown of Caesar.

The most noteworthy *candélabre* of the period is the one made by the silversmith Auguste for Napoleon during the hundred-day period between his return from Elba and his subsequent exile to St. Helena. This magnificent *surtout de table* has a tapering cylindrical stem mounted on a high domed base. The top of the stem merges into an ovoid vase from which radiate the four acanthus scrolled cornucopia candle branches, the mouths of which are fitted with candle sockets. The finer ends of the cornucopias terminate in swans mounted around the central vase, and above the swans is the fifth and central candle socket. Elaborately scrolled acanthus curl within the curve of the branches and there is finely cut decoration on the base.

It is typical of Empire design in every way.

Just as Thomire and Percier dominated the work in silver and bronze and were noted for their lighting fittings and clocks, so Auguste and Biennais excelled in silver plate, the latter being noted for his use of the double eagle and for his *candélabre*, *torchères* and mantle ornaments; and Auguste made a wonderfully conceived *surtout de table* consisting of thirty-one pieces, which included twenty-two three- or four-light candélabres mounted amongst fountains, temples and altars all mounted on *bronze doré* and decorated with reliefs and statues. There were also different coloured marble, cameos, agate, alabaster and porphyry to add colour amongst the superb metalwork. This fine treasure was a gift to Napoleon from Charles IV of Spain.

Grand *lustres* of French or Bohemian crystal held pride of place among the fine furnishings. Many cut-glass arms amid festoons of buttons, swags and strings of glittering crystal, held tall tapering candles whose flickering flame sent rainbows of colour darting through the draped crystal. The typical and popular Empire 'balloon' was formed around a wide, gold or silver hoop suspended from the ceiling on a rod. From the ceiling-decoration depended strings of graduated crystal buttons, draping downwards and outwards to terminate around the circumference of the hoop, thus forming the 'pavilion' of the fitting. Below the hoop, strings of graduated buttons are gathered together around a small central plate and in this way form the basket or balloon beneath the pavilion. Swags and crystal pendants fell gracefully from projecting scrolls. Candles or oil cups burned minutely within the framework of the

29   Empire 'balloon', c.1815.

crystal, and candle arms, springing out-wards from the circumference of the hoop, held tall wax candles (Plate 29).

A typical lantern was of cast iron or bronze, circular and with vertical, slotted grill forming the top band, while glazed sides tapered towards the base which terminated on scrolls. These scrolls were mounted on a base which fitted onto the candle post. The top of the lantern was encircled by anthemion fretwork and eagles, while the vented chimney was topped by a flaming crest or an eagle.

The old Roman type of hanging lamp came back into use but was now highly sophisticated, in metal and decorated with sphinxes, goats' heads, swags, eagles and winged lions. Some were made for hanging and others were mounted on standards and were known as the *lampadaire*.

By this time a great many lamps were in use among the lower classes but few of them seem to have been worthy of improvement, and probably the most convenient design originated from England in the shape of Birmingham button manufacturer John Miles' oil-tight font, which could survive agitation without spillage; and as the rank and file continued to use their candles, their pan lamps and their rush lights, deterioriation was taking place at top government level.

The era ended as it had begun, in a complexity of diplomatic success and defeat, including the celebrated defeat of 1812 in Russia; Napoleon's resignation at *Fontainbleau* in 1814, and his final surrender to the British after Waterloo in March 1815.

The period is contemporary with the later part of the reign of George III in England, and includes the Regency of the Prince of Wales. It is noted for its departure from the styles of Louis XVI in favour of a more formal line in *le style Directoire*. The Empire introduced the shaded table lamp, the C-shaped cornucopia candle arm, and the more extensive use of cupids. Mirrors and lanterns, topped by the eagle were also characteristic of the period, and Carcel oil lamps made their appearance. In crystal, the giant 'balloon' fitting provided a new status symbol for the wealthy, and the use of black figured prominently in decoration.

With the death of Napoleon in May 1821, died also the great personal influence which marked the most fascinating rule of decoration and manner which we readily appreciate in *le style Empire*.

1815–1850
The events between 1815 and 1850, which

embrace the reigns of Louis XVIII (1815–24), Charles X (1824–30), and Louis Phillippe (1830–48), are not always accorded significance, but they do, in fact, represent an important transitional period from the grace of the fallen Empire to the fall from grace of furnishing styles which mark the second half of the century.

For example, by about 1820, the Empire style of furniture had been superseded, and those pieces which had been discarded found their way to the less ostentatious domains of rich merchants and middle-class citizens. Much of what remained was actually stripped of its Empire appendages in an effort to disguise its origins. An example of this was to be found in the treatment of the handsome cylindrical coach lamp so prized by the Empire. Its scrolls, eagles and fretwork were removed to leave only the basic cylindrical form surmounted by an unadorned smoke vent, and this was the model which appeared in England in about 1830.

Born out of the indecision over originating a new style of furnishing the era commenced a succession of revivals which included Gothic and Renaissance, and a return to the styles of Louis XV and XVI, the modifications of which may sometimes cause confusion for the unpractised student. The principal interpretation of the style in Paris, London and Berlin underwent modification and simplification to such an extent that by the half-century it had become known as *Biedermeier* style, which loosely describes an article as 'pretending to be something it is not.'

The Argand lamp now became the principal source of illumination. Candlesticks, candelabra and chandeliers had their candle sockets removed or otherwise adapted to allow for the fitting of the new oil lamps. Chandelier arms terminated in the metal basket required to carry the oil font of larger lamps, and they had glass chimneys to steady the flame and decorated glass globes to diffuse the light. One hanging oil lamp in ormolu and black metal, shows the return of the S-scroll arm which supports the oil font surmounted by the burner and globe (Plate 30).

30 Lampadaire, *c.1840*.

If we are to find a Charles X lighting fitting, it might well be the Student Lamp. This, in the form most familiar to us was introduced just prior to 1830. It was made with a central brass post fitted to a heavy circular base and topped by a carrying loop. An oil font for colza oil was fitted on a central collar so as to gravity-feed the lamp reservoir mounted on an arm opposite and slightly below the level of the font. The Argand wick was protected by a glass chimney and over this rested a circular gallery which held a green glass shade to reduce the glare and direct the light downwards (Plate 31).

On the introduction of this highly efficient table lamp, the old *lucerna* which had been in use for many years, rapidly lost its popularity. However, the shaded Empire table candlestick continued in use until it had been entirely superseded by the oil lamp.

By 1830–5, table lamps, floor standards, wall brackets and hanging fittings adopted the oil principle, and for the first time it became possible to produce repetition models in quantity for general marketing purposes.

The colza oil Moderatore lamp, introduced in 1836, had a pretty decorated standard base as the font and inside this was housed a clockwork mechanism for forcing the heavy oil up to the wick, a method not replaced until the introduction of paraffin lamp-oil in the 1860s.

There was still the possibility of the widespread use of gas for lighting and cooking, but not much enthusiasm from the authorities for its adoption. The French pioneer of gas-lighting was Philippe Lebon, who in 1802 had supervised the installation

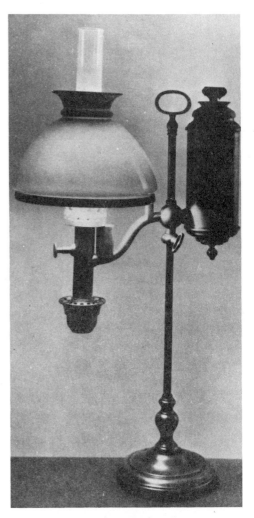

31   Student lamp, c.1830.

of gas lights in a house in Paris, and had subsequently secured a patent from the French government for 'the art of producing light from wood, ignited in closed vessels.'

Although he made scant progress without financial backing, his theory was sound enough to have established a workable system on a large scale, but his death at the hands of thieves in 1804 terminated further activity in that direction.

But Lebon's attempts to popularise gas had not been in vain, for his demonstrations had been keenly attended by a determined contemporary named Friedrich Albrecht Winzer, a German who had no mechanical or scientific skills, but found a compelling urge to further the case for gas lighting in a courageous one-man campaign.

Finding no interest in the subject on the Continent, Winzer changed his name to Frederick Albert Winsor, and departed for England where he hoped his reception would be more favourable.

But life was not entirely candles and oil lamps – or even gas. An astonishing device for attaching batteries to a pair of carbon rods and causing a spark to bridge the gap between them had been introduced from England, and was now occupying the minds of eager inventors. The arc-light, as it was called, was fed by chemical cells, and its brilliant spark would light large areas almost as brightly as sunlight, except that it died suddenly when the batteries failed to maintain the power or the carbon rods burned away.

Between 1841–44, several streets were experimentally lit by these battery-powered arc lamps, and the Paris Opéra enjoyed the excitement of the new invention in 1846, but due to the short life of the batteries and the inefficiency of the control gear, the scheme was rejected as impracticable, and everyone returned their attention to candles and oil lamps once again.

With the growing development of domestic gas as a lighting and heating medium, France of the 1840s began to speculate on the possibilities of the English gas lighting system becoming a powerful rival to their existing and beloved candle-light.

At this point, since it no longer serves the purpose of this story to proceed further, we shall leave France to Louis Phillippe, during whose reign the wheel of fashion had turned full cycle.

CHAPTER THREE

Spain

With the Bay of Biscay on the North, the Atlantic on the West and the Mediterranean on the South, Spain provides an unusually long coastline, which, from earliest times, invited the attention of travellers, adventurers and pirates alike; so that a considerable foreign influence infiltrated the principalities, few as they were, in this austere, barren country.

But there had never been the strong influence of a great city such as London, Rome or Paris, for the old trade routes were uneasy or unprofitable, and even a potentially valuable connection with France was severed by the Pyrenees, and in a country whose communications depended upon the horse and the ox-cart, travelling the narrow tracks, there was no encouragement for the merchants to venture further than was necessary for the selling of their wares.

Spain had once formed an important part of the Roman Empire, but after the Decline the country fell variously to the ransacking tribes that roamed Europe in search of plunder, shelter and food; and in this quest

no one race was more successful than the Moors, who overran the Peninsular, established themselves as a permanent and powerful community, and remained so until their expulsion in 1609 allowed other designs to dominate their long established principles.

Nevertheless, their influence is to be found throughout the decorative history of Spain, and lighting fittings received as much attention as did the rest of the wonderful furnishings that developed under the wealthy Caliphs for the enjoyment of the ruling classes.

In those parts remote from the industry of the big towns, the old Roman hand lamp, the *velon*, still had a functional place in every household, and the familiar open oil pan with pinched wick-spout remained an essential device for lighting in the kitchen. In Spain, this useful oil-burning lamp was called the *candil*, having its equivalents in the French *candile* and the Italian *lucerna*.

The *palmatoria* was a hand candlestick made or iron; the *lampara* was a hanging fitting for candles, and the *corona de luz* was a wrought iron hanging chandelier suspended on chains from a hook in the ceiling. The candlestick was a *candelabro,* and candelabras were *candelabros;* the iron standard to hold a lantern was a *torchere;* a *candelabro formando lirios* was a *candelabro* surrounded by tiers of delicately formed lilies fashioned in iron.

The *lampada* was an oil or grease-burning lamp; the *farole,* a lantern for use in the hallway, on the stairs or in the room centre; the *final,* a lantern for use at the end or sides of a room, and the *faroles atorreonados* was an ornate lantern with turrets around the top.

Of this impressive selection, it was the *candil,* the *palmatoria* and the small hanging lantern – the *farole* – that comprised the lighting facilities of the average house or cottage, for these were functional heirlooms that were handed down through the generations together with the furniture and cooking pots.

Because of the absence of a really efficient illuminant, lighting devices were limited to the use of oil or grease, or candles and pitch-rope; and in consequence, the purely functional pieces remained simple and primitive, while luxurious lighting devices were made so by elaboration of decoration and multiple light sources, as is evident in the *candelabro multiple,* an iron pyramid-shaped framework for hanging, and having several prickets fitted upright along the sides of the triangle.

In contrast with the harsh conditions of life in the North and the enforced use of splints and grease pans, the comfortably accommodated Moors amused themselves with little lamps mounted on gimbals within a hollow brass ball which was delicately pierced and embossed with designs. These lamps came originally from China or Persia, and were of two kinds; the Chafing Ball for warming the hands, and the Rolling Lamp for rolling along the ground, the object of the game being to see who among the contestants could roll his lamp the faster without extinguishing the flame.

As a refinement, the Moors used the lamps for burning perfume and hung them around the neck on coloured cords or gold chain, or used them after the manner of a censer about their lavish interiors, so that exotic aromas pervaded the atmosphere.

The period styles of Spain are often misunderstood as they overlap by a considerable margin and are open to confusion, especially as the Moorish influence in the South lasted for something like nine hundred years and survived the introduction of many other period styles during that time; but without becoming heavily involved in detail we can briefly account for the periods as we see them in terms of lighting history.

The Moorish period (710–1609) is alternatively known as the *Hispano-Arabe,* or Spanish-Arabian period, the middle period of which brings to mind the superb Alhambraic palaces of the 1250s, and, of course, those of the Mohammedans.

In the great hanging lanterns, pierced and engraved by the Moors after ancient Persian designs, one feels the power of their ingenuity and the scope of their craftsmanship, characteristics which so greatly impressed visitors from abroad. These lanterns were made of pierced brass, silver or bronze, and often of coloured or gilded tin. The open fretwork-type of design produced a dancing silhouette of arabesque patterning surrounding the flame, which is the key to the subtlety of Moorish lantern making. The object was to exploit the play of light from within; to silhouette the intricacies of a pierced design so that when a lantern was set close to a wall or drape an intriguing shadow pattern was projected for all to admire and enjoy.

The term 'arabesque' is used to identify the leafy scrollwork so often associated with Arab workmanship, although it was originally of Persian invention, but like so much of Persian craft making its appearance in the West at an early date, it was incorrectly attributed to Arab origins since the Moors were such masters of the art.

The typical Moorish lantern is pierced all over in these arabesque designs, with window-like openings and a mosque-like dome top and bottom.

The *Romanico* or *Romanesco* period (Eleventh to Fifteenth Century) is noted for the high standard of wrought iron work which Spain had perfected even before the Fourteenth Century. From Catalan, near the Pyrenees, two workers of outstanding skill, Suñnol and Blay, were contracted to work on Nôtre Dame in Paris. Their *candelabros* and *candelabroa* were made with delicately formed lilies, an influence of the French *Romanesque* which had made itself apparent after the defeat of the Moors at Toledo in 1085, and which lasted until the Thirteenth Century. A typical Catalan table candlestick was a large circular or rectangular drip pan with scolloped or turreted edging, mounted on simple bracket feet. Prickets or sockets or a mixture of both were provided for the candles.

Southern Spain enjoyed a standard of luxury unparalleled elsewhere in Europe at that time. Interiors were spacious and lavishly draped with beautiful textiles. Furniture was rectangular, decorated and wax polished, perfume burners on silken cords swung like pendulums in every room, brightly coloured tiles and mosaics covered the floors, and ornamental fountains trickled musically in the courtyards.

Dinanderie candlesticks, decorated with *champlevé* or *cloisonné* enamelling were introduced during the Twelfth Century, and remained among the ornaments of the house for two centuries or more, while even yet the rich Caliphs reclined on their silk cushions amid the splendour of their achievements.

During the *Gótico* (Gothic) period of 1250–1500, the Moors suffered considerable political and spiritual defeats. They had been forcibly divided after centuries of conflict with the Christians, and many had retreated to Africa leaving the large territories formerly ruled by the Caliphs to be subdued by new rulers. The remaining Moors established their kingdom in Granada in 1200, from which they continued the battle for superiority. In a series of wars the Christians slowly recovered possession of the Peninsula, and ended the long conflict when Granada, the last Moorish stronghold, surrendered in 1492.

Many of the Moors, struggling to maintain the roots of their old civilisation in Spain, adopted the Christian religion, and under its moral and spiritual protection continued their artistic contributions to the making of lanterns, candle holders, lamps and street furniture. Furthermore, they understood the art of Gothic decoration, and developed it with an admixture of Moorish style, which produced the beautiful *Hispano-Moresco* period between 1250 and 1609, by which latter date they had been entirely banished from the kingdom.

During the *Gótico* period, lanterns were made of iron or tin, with either an open, scrolled top or a heavy dome. Both had lily and crown motifs from sometime during the Eleventh Century, but mostly the crown.

Barcelona and Toledo produced large quantities of glassware, and among their products were chandeliers, candlesticks and lantern glass, which now began to take the place of the old Moorish pierced metalwork.

The Fourteenth Century brought the finest of the tripod floor standards in sizes up to seven feet tall, bearing prickets or sockets for large candles, and with wide drip pans supported on brackets.

Multi-light standards were fitted with one or more hoops to hold the candles. The *corona de luz* – crown of light – was a hanging fitting, the simplest being made of flat strap-iron in the form of a hoop with pans and sockets around its circumference. Cross-beams, the main supporting members of the hoop, were turned upwards at the edge of the hoop to form the *fleurs-de-lis* as decoration, and the whole fitting was suspended from chains.

The extensive, almost extreme, use of floral decoration superimposed upon the Gothic character, lead to the *Gótico-florido* of 1492–1700, and lasted well beyond the Renaissance.

Culture and luxury had for long been an inheritance from the Moors, but as feudalism diminished there grew a general desire for individual achievement, and with the advancement of design, individual skills emerged to be recognised on their merits.

By then the Renaissance had filtered into Spain from Italy, and the Spanish *Renacimiento* (1500–1600) provided the age of splendour which glorified the reign of Charles V.

In attempting to cultivate the wishes of their conquerors, those Moorish craftsmen who had elected to remain under the Christian faith, evolved a style of working that was half-Moorish, half-European, and which was afterwards called *Mudéjar* (Moorish Renaissance) which helped to account for another important concept of design between 1500 and 1610. The *Mudéjar* lantern had graceful, elongated sides with still the hints of the old mosque lamp, but with a more geometric approach, especially in the treatment of the glass panels which were sometimes elaborated with superimposed patterns.

The true art of lantern-making originated in the Sixteenth Century, although past centuries of experiment and success must have preceded it, for perfection is not achieved in one first attempt. Silver and gold, beloved of Spain, had for long balanced the brass and bronze work of the Moors, but iron and tin were worked with the same delicacy as the more precious metals.

Flat bottom lanterns were set upon tables and pedestals within the house, and hanging lanterns were suspended either from wall brackets or from the ceiling on colourful silken cords. The geometric design of these lanterns carried through several other periods, occasionally bearing their decorative influences embodied in their main design; the pierced arabesques of the Moors, the bold ornament of the Baroque, the rectangular shape of the Renaissance or the turreted galleries of the Mudéjars.

Within the broad outline of the *Renacimiento* two separate and distinct interpretations are to be found; the first in *el estile plateresco* (1500–1550), a term coined from *platero* meaning silversmith.

The preponderance of silver and gold, violently looted from the ancient civilisations of the Americas, encouraged the free use of these precious metals for ornamental fittings, and the term *Plateresco* was intended to identify the period of this work.

Finely wrought ironwork had gold leaf beaten in, or molten gold applied to the surface to produce patterns or highlights. *Candelabros* and other fittings of the period were also extravagantly finished in gold or silver, but mostly in gold.

Glass lamps from Barcelona were either plain or coloured, sometimes amber, sometimes green. Hanging brass lamps from Italy, sanctuary lamps from Persia and bronze chandeliers from the Netherlands, blended with the newly formed decorations, while native-made floor standards of gilded iron reached as high as eight feet.

The second interpretation is *el estilo Herrera* (1556–1600), named after the architect who had studied under Michaelangelo. Silver was delicately worked and lavishly used during this period, the most notable silversmith being Juan de Arphe, who worked in the Greco-Roman style after Cellini. His most beautiful work is to

32 Farol *lantern, Early Seventeenth Century.*

be found in sanctuary lamps, altar candlesticks, church candelabra and ewers.

The Sixteenth Century lantern was rectangular and glass panelled, becoming hexagonal in the latter years. Long arched panels framed on either side by slender columns, supported an elaborate domed top and rested on a domed base. Pierced vents in the scroll work of the dome allowed

33 Final *lantern, Seventeenth/Nineteenth Century.*

old Moorish styles began to disappear from new designs as the base became narrower and the lantern tapered from top to bottom. One such final lantern is rectangular with typical downward taper and has four glass windows, each window being divided into smaller panes. The corners of the body are decorated by applied leaf work; the top is composed of S-scrolls overlaid with acanthus leaf supporting a simple royal crown, in the centre of which is the suspension hook for the chain. The bottom is attached to double C-shaped scrolls terminating around an acanthus finial from which depends a coloured cord tassel (Plate 33).

An identical lantern top could be mounted on an iron tripod standard, when it became the *torchère farol,* a lantern for use anywhere in the house. In earlier models the stem was fairly plain, being of square section iron, relieved halfway along by a simple scrolled decoration. The squat tripod foot was surrounded by scrolls at the base of the stem, and at the top, the coloured cord tassel of the lantern draped down to add a touch of colour to the gilded ironwork.

The most popular design of late Seventeenth Century standards was the spiral-twist of the lower section of the shaft and the high voluted tripod foot. Central knops were of openwork acanthus foliage, and the upper stem was decorated with lightly chased formal patterns. Lanterns were of gilded tin with clear glass.

But fine garments, painted furniture, silk cushions and ornate lanterns were not for the rank and file, and even some noblemen were not so resplendent that gold and silver were commonplace in their homes. In the wealthy houses, hanging lamps

smoke and heat to escape from the candle or oil lamp within.

Some lanterns were made entirely of tin, polychromed and pierced all over with patterns. A turret of small cut shapes ran around the hexagonal top and the lily motif was freely used (Plate 32).

In the late Seventeenth Century both the vertical and the wide base outline of the provided light for the dining table; hoops of candles hung from chains in the communal hall, and wrought iron candlesticks sufficed for the bed chambers.

Not much of note has survived to complete the image of those bygone days, especially as the reign of Philip II (1555–98) did nothing to enhance the splendour of Spanish craft. His encouragement of the terrible Inquisition cast a shadow over the land when practically everything of beauty was destroyed and every citizen went in fear of torture or death. There perished an alarming amount of precious and magnificent furnishings which should have numbered among the national treasures.

The severest of ironwork survived the destruction; newly-made lighting fittings were relatively plain, and many of the older, more decorative fittings were stripped of their applied decoration and painted black.

Generally speaking, the passageways, staircases and most large rooms were lighted by conical iron torches set in brackets on the wall and burning tarred rope or fat. Such torches were demountable so that they could be carried to light the way through those sections of the premises not accorded a permanent light. The simple candlestick, with one or more prickets, served the bedchambers and servants quarters, that is, if the servants were allowed candles, for they were not plentiful and were hand-made.

The unhappy plight of the country at the time of Philip's death is important, since the release from the austere morbidity of his wretched régime lead to the most extravagant of all the period styles.

The *Barroco* (1600–1750), is no doubt the most representative of Spanish decoration. Carvings were gilded or coloured in red, blue and gold. Costly fabrics draped the walls and arches. Furniture was lacquered in red, ivory, white and green, and inlaid with ebony, tortoise-shell, bronze or silver. Upholstery came in quilted fabrics, velvet, leather or rich brocades with tassels and fringes.

Lighting fittings were again coloured and ornamented, reviving the use of the lily, the griffin and the dragon. A bracket of the period would be attached to a tall iron backplate which supported before it a grinning dragon with wings aspread and his tail curling around the post on which he stands. In outstretched claws he supports

34 *Dragon bracket, c.1700.*

35   Corona de luz, *Eighteenth Century.*

supported on a single iron rod rising from a base with four large pad feet. Four deep-cup pans on baluster posts were supported off the centre stem by horizontal brackets which secured the candle posts top and bottom.

The flat bottom lantern became more common, and more geometric in its design. Whereas the previous lanterns had been elaborate with pierced patterns or applied decoration, the seventeenth-century Baroque lantern emphasised the area of glass rather than the framework, and the principle of that intention was brought to perfection in the *Barroco* period.

An extant example has a large rectangular, gilded tin body or framework of

a semi-circular bracket with a lily motif projecting from its centre. Each end of the bracket bears a vertical post and a deep cup holding the candle socket. The wall plate, candle posts and cups are black, but the dragon is finely enamelled in red, gold and green (Plate 34).

The useful innovation of having deep, basin-like pans to receive the melting wax and charred snuff was soon adopted on other candle holders and is characteristic of the period.

A four-light *corona de luz* was suspended on twisted iron rods from a centre ceiling hook and the deep-cup pans were mounted on strap-iron scrolls which formed the body of the fitting (Plate 35).

Candle sockets replaced the prickets in later models.

A simple floor-standing *candelabro* was

36   Barroco *lantern case, Eighteenth Century.*

complex geometric design, set upon scrolled feet and looking something like a large, glass-sided birds cage.

Bevelled glass windows form the four larger panels whose corners are not carried out to a formal right angle but are cut across so as to connect the large panels by small vertical panels which give the lantern an eight-sided appearance (Plate 36).

Lanterns of this type were made for hanging as well as for standing, and the hanging lantern of the Seventeenth/ Eighteenth Centuries had many glass panels, but revived the pierced dome top and bottom of the Mudéjar and Renaissance influence.

The most widely exported, and perhaps the most interesting of the eighteenth-century designs was the geometric, eight-pointed star, known as the Andalusian Star. This was a fine achievement of design and craftsmanship in which shaped glass panes were combined with gilded tin framework in the form of a star. The centre of the body was an octagonal glass chamber for the candle or lamp. The star points radiated around the chamber, and the uppermost point terminated in a ventilator formed by tin foliage which also enclosed the suspension loop, while a lower finial point held coloured tassels.

Lanterns with twelve or more points were common, and although originals are rare, authentic versions are still produced for those who appreciate the style of the Andalusian Star.

Lanterns mounted on decorated poles helped to light the way out of doors, or were used along passageways and staircases. There was little in the way of street

37 Lampara cornoa, *c.1750*.

lighting, so that lanterns fitted by the entrance to a building were particularly important to those obliged to travel after dusk.

Outstanding among the artists of the era was the architect Churrigura from whom originated the *estilo Churrigueresco* of 1650 at the time when the Baroque was at its height. So great an influence was Churrigura's use of abundant ornament and strong colour that his style persisted into the Eighteenth Century.

Candelabros and *lamparas*, made of silver, wood, bronze or iron, were poly-chromed or gilded in the finest manner. Heavy scrolling, floral motifs and acanthus leaves were accompanied by cherubs and paw feet supports. A two-tier *corona de luz* of the late period bears ten scrolled candle arms around the lower body and five arms radiating around the centre of the shaft, the top of which terminates in outward springing leafwork. Overlaid foliage along the candle arms, shows, perhaps, a French influence, but patterns on the body are Moorish (Plate 37).

The Spanish appreciation of Moorish-Renaissance continued to impress itself on lantern making for many years, and one type of six-sided lantern, made in the Nineteenth Century, tapers downward from a heavy domed top attached to slim, tapering pillars, each surmounted by the *fleurs-de-lis*. The window tops are flattened ogee arches of the type familiar in English Tudor architecture, and a ventilator projects from each section of the six-sided dome after the style of their Fifteenth Century ancestors, A brass sanctuary lamp of the Eighteenth Century still conserves the character of Moorish work in its deep basin, its pierced designs and the elaborate openwork suspension chains beloved of Moorish craftsmen.

In identifying Spanish lanterns, there are three rules of design which are typical of the periods. The Moorish lantern has a domed top and its sides slope outwards to a domed base. The Gothic lantern is equilateral with vertical patterns; and the Renaissance lantern is wide at the top and tapers downward to the base. The Baroque lantern repeats many designs of the Seventeenth Century, with domes and turrets, scrolls and crowns, coloured glass and stars. The flat bottom, geometric lantern case is a prominent product of the period and the Andalusian Star maintains the method of working with tin and glass well into the Eighteenth Century.

Influences from other European countries infiltrated into Spain during this century as her own mastery of the arts began to diminish. At first, furnishings in the French style made no great impression on the nation which had for so long commanded its own inheritance of beauty and skill, particularly since the French enjoyed no friendly corner of the Spanish heart. Nevertheless, Spain was to become noted for her reproduction of classical originals and one can see late developments of the Rococo in furniture, and in the adoption of the *bombé* swell of the period.

In lighting fittings there is a distinct overlay of foliage on the Moorish framework, giving a charming character to the

38   *Empire bracket, c.1790.*

early Spanish interpretation of the rococo; and even *le style Empire* becomes evident in the cornucopia-shaped candle arms and popular motifs of Louis XVI designers.

One wall bracket in the French style had a tall backplate arising from a tapering urn overflowing with floral decoration, on which rested a cameo of a female head against a coloured background. The design was surmounted by leaves and the popular anthemion display. Flat pans and decorated candle cups were supported on C-scroll arms (Plate 38).

Behind the grand facade of wealth and candlelight, the oil lamp had been slowly penetrating the more progressive homesteads, but it was not until 1750 or so that a number of decorated float-wick lamps came in from France to inspire the Spanish lamp makers to better deeds. They made stems of baluster or vase shape and fitted them with discs of tin supported on cork floats which trailed the wick through their centres into the oil below. Glass workers in Barcelona, Catalan and Maiorca, made cylindrical chimneys to fit over the wick to keep the flame steady.

About 1777, the flat cotton wick, which had been invented by Leger in France, came to Spain to provide the first improvement in oil-burning devices for centuries, and this was almost superseded during the early 1780s by the introduction of whale oil, an enterprising by-product of the flourishing whaling industry of the South Pacific. The whale oil lamp was in itself a unique type of burner, inasmuch as that the cover or lid was screwed into the font, making the lamp oil-tight and non-spillable. The principle of the design was to be found in the 'agitable' lamp which had

been invented in England in 1787, and since it was ideal for use aboard ship as well as in domestic quarters, it was readily adopted for both land and marine use, being provided with one, two or three vertical wick tubes, mounted in the cover at a slight angle so that the oil seeped up to the wick more easily than would have been the case had the tubes been upright. In this form they are called whale oil lamps, although other types of base may also be whale-oil burners.

Whale oil was cheaper than most other illuminants, but it was odious and viscous, sometimes being difficult to burn unless it had been specially processed to make it more manageable, when it was referred to as 'edulcorated' whale oil.

Sea elephant oil was much cheaper and burned brightly without smoke, but as both whale and sea elephant oil had to be brought from the Pacific they were beyond the means of the average citizen, who continued to use the *palmatoria* and the *candil,* or the small decorated pottery float-lamp called the *mariposa.*

In contrast to the small lighting devices employed by the majority, mosque lamps were often made on a large scale, probably to ensure their significance in the vastness of the mosque, but the most common hanging lamps of the Nineteenth Century were of more rational proportions than the earlier models, being made after the style of the typical pointed dome of a minaret, and measuring about thirty-six inches from top to bottom.

They originated in the Near East and found favour along the principal trade routes to India, Persia, Turkey, Cairo and the Western Mediterranean; not necessarily in

39 Mosque lamp, Nineteenth Century.

places of worship, but often occupying pride of place amid carved screens, silk cushions, Cordova leathers and the perfume-burners of splendid rooms.

This type of lamp was made of brass, embossed with designs and pierced with patterns, leaving hardly any undecorated surface. The base of the dome was joined to a lower body which flared outwards and finished with a flat bottom to which was fitted a number of cylindrical glass oil fonts projecting downwards and at a slight angle from the vertical. The fonts were charged with a measure of oil floated on two or three inches of water and contained a fibre or cotton wick supported on a glass rod in the centre. Long, decorated chains suspended the lamp from the ceiling or wall bracket, from which position they shed their light from many wavering flames (Plate 39).

However, it was not until the gravity-feed system of the colza oil lamps of the 1840s had been superseded by the introduction of paraffin in the 1860s that the design of oil-burning lamps radically changed and brought a brighter, cheaper means of lighting to the country that still cherished its Moorish lamps and its *candils*.

CHAPTER FOUR

England

A small block of stone, hollowed with the aid of sharpened flint and filled with animal fat feeding a moss wick, was the principal source of artificial light for at least a thousand years before the first Roman expedition touched the English shores (Plate 40); and salmonoid fish, dried and set alight at the mouth, sea-shells burning fish oil, or the oily body of a dead stormy petrel stuffed with a fibre wick, had additionally served coastal dwellers for even longer.

40 Stone lamp.

Rush torches crackled and flared to lay bare the first nights of the Roman invasion, an epic which lead to a compromise of rule which lasted for 400 years (A.D. 43–410) and which brought to the islanders an astonishing new culture and a profitable trade.

The Britons had for long been accustomed to using grease-burning lamps made either of stone, chalk or metal, and the introduction of the Roman hand lamp – primarily an oil-burning device – added to their limited selection of lights. There would certainly have been difficulty with lighting such lamps when employing grease as the illuminant, since fats depend upon the warmth of the lamp and the heat of the flame to liquify the area around the wick. As clay is a poor conductor of heat it would have been necessary to warm the lamp over a fire before it became possible to light the wick.

The quantity so far excavated from the ruins of Roman Briton indicate the widespread use of these little clay lamps, so no doubt the supply of burning oil was no great problem for the resourceful Roman Empire.

The bronze hand lamp, decorated or plainly made, was a sophisticated version of the clay lamp, and shed its small light in corridors and rooms of the fine villas which soon dominated the architecture of the principal towns and cities; and tall bronze tripod standards holding dishes of burning oil were the first street lights ever to be seen by the Britons.

By far the most domestically useful device was the open top iron pan with a wick channel. Burning either oil or grease, it could be hung from a roof beam or wall bracket by means of a wire hoop handle in the simpler types or by a spiked rod in the more robust models. This was probably the device described in the Bible as a 'cruse', which came down to us in history centuries later as the 'crusie' or 'cruzy'.

Sanctuary lamps, primarily intended for places of worship and coming from the East, burned steadily in halls, private apartments or beneath the portico of many a classic villa, for there was no distinction between domestic and religious usage.

So much time and destruction separates us from that remarkable four-hundred-year period that only fragments of information remain to guide us in our reconstruction of the ancient past, and whatever had been left by the Romans in the haste of their evacuation was plundered or destroyed in successive raids by the Saxons, the Danes, and the Normans.

Over a thousand years were to pass before the wonders of the old Roman Empire would be seen again in the art of the Renaissance, but meanwhile the various people who migrated from the Continent to become the new race of Anglo-Saxons, developed their own skills and established the Anglo-Saxon period which lasted until the Eleventh Century. Among the simple lighting devices of the time they made decorated pottery saucers which became known as 'Saxon dishes', and there were hanging lamps of stone or pottery called 'cressets'.

Hanging candle holders were made of crossed beams of wood, a spike being driven upwards through the beams to hold the candles. There was also the 'Saxon wheel', a cart wheel suspended horizontally on chains or ropes and having around its circumference a number of spikes upon which to impale the candles.

Renowned for their work in metals, the Anglo-Saxons soon refashioned the wooden wheel as an iron hoop, omitting the spokes and providing sockets instead of prickets. The wooden cross beams were also copied in iron, and there were hanging fittings and candle holders of silver, bronze, copper and silver-gilt, decorated with coloured enamels, ivory and precious stones.

By the Seventh Century, the hanging Saxon dishes were heavily ornamented with colourful medalions, foliage and animal motifs, and they became so widely noted that Anglo-Saxon craftsmen in Rome, in the Eight–Ninth Centuries, were making hanging lamps of copper and silver.

The majority of people used rush-lights, splints or fire-pans, having little use for anything more advanced, for their time was divided between working on the land, taking up arms on behalf of their lords and masters or fighting off invading armies – not always with success.

At the time of their Conquest in 1066 the Normans found a country wealthy in gold, silver, tin and copper, and an aristocracy that was largely ready and willing to co-operate in order to retain their positions in England and their lands in France.

That the French language was readily adopted accounts for the fact that most lighting fittings of the period were known by their French names; the *chandelier* was a candle holder, either for the table, for hanging, or for the wall, the *bobèche* was the drip pan, the *roue de fer* was an iron wheel fitted with candle sockets, and the *bougeoir* was a small candlestick.

The Saxon dishes of the Seventh Century and the silver hanging lamps of the Ninth Century gave way to imported Limoges enamel candlesticks and to the jaunty, strutting *dinanderie,* whose popularity throughout Europe knew no equal for several centuries.

Hardly anything of note has survived the early period of English lighting history, except for one remarkable piece of ecclesiastical work of the Norman-Romanesque period (1066–1189). That is the Gloucester Candlestick, a curiously beautiful work of art dating from the year 1110.

It measures twenty-three inches from the foot to the top of the pricket, and stands on a base eight inches in diameter, and is made of richly gilt bell-metal, its three components being held together by an iron rod through the centre. It is the sharpened end of this rod that protrudes through the grease pan to form the pricket.

Here is the combination of several foreign influences. In silhouette, the candlestick has the raised foot, the knopped stem and wide grease pan of Limoges character.

Each foot of the base is raised and set with the peculiar squat, striding character of the typical *dinanderie* candlestick.

Down each of these feet is a reptile, fashioned with characteristic attitude, its head extended and jaws eagerly agape. The body of the candlestick comprises a complex mobility of human figures and monsters, writhing and groping their

41   *The Gloucester Candlestick, c.1110.*

individual paths towards the grease pan which is upheld by three dragons. Between the gargoyle-like humans and their chimerical companions there is the occasional leaf and scroll which anticipates the Gothic period of 1189–1509, unless it derives from earlier Continental influences.

As virtually no domestic plate now exists earlier than the Fourteenth Century the Gloucester Candlestick has to be the sole example by which probable standards of the era may be judged, for such perfection is not achieved in a single attempt (Plate 41).

Most candlesticks of the period were simple and made variously in iron, bronze or copper and a copper-zinc mixture called latten. Brass was not the highly polished product known today, but a dull, mellow colour subject to tarnishing, for which reason it was either protected by frequent oiling or had to be painted or gilded. Wood, hewn by the axe, fashioned by the knife and joined by dowels or iron nails, formed many an individual creation in lanterns and candlesticks.

The lantern evolved from the need to protect the candle flame from the draught, and anciently translucent sections of animal horn were used for the windows, and the term 'lanthorn' was used to describe this type of lighting device. Better lanterns were made of tin, iron, brass and leather, and some might have had glass windows, but only a proportion of the available light could have been transmitted because the glass in those days was not transparent, but either a chalky white with almost clear patches, or was tinted green or brown.

Hanging lights were rare. The Gothic *corona* – a hoop – held either a series of small glass or metal oil fonts called *gabatte*, or candles on prickets. Some churches retained the ancient *polycandelon*, a flat circular plate suspended on chains and bearing glass float-lamps set into slots around its circumference.

The only positive design in evidence by the end of the Twelfth Century was the baluster form of the solid brass chandeliers from the Netherlands, with their heavy sphere-weighted body and S-scroll candle arms, and these were used mostly in churches until the Fourteenth Century, when the appeal of their design brought them into domestic use.

Most churches had, built into the stone walls, small basins called cressets. They were not used for Holy water or for rinsing the hands before prayer as is sometimes supposed, but were oil-burning float-lamps, by the meagre light of which people came to pay their devotions.

An article of church furniture which was also called a cresset was the simple iron cage placed over the body or tomb of a knight. The most simple cresset of this type had only four candles, but the elaborate ones had eight or more according to choice and cost.

Another cresset was the iron cage – fire basket – used out of doors to light the way at night. A variation of designs allowed for a flexibility of purpose; some being mounted on an iron pole partly driven into the ground as support, others being made as wall-mounting brackets, while others were made to hang from a projecting arm on the corner of a building. They were filled with coils of pitched rope that burned brightly for several hours.

After the Black Death of 1349, craftsmen

were few since whole villages were left unpopulated, and out of the two-and-a-half-million survivors of the plague only relatively few artistic workers were able eventually to establish their trades in the recovering capital.

In 1466, Phillipe le Bon attacked and destroyed the Flanders town of Dinant, the source of the popular *dinanderie* candlesticks, and many of the fleeing craftsmen took refuge in England, where they were readily absorbed into the societies of smiths and designers; a happy unity which further popularised the Flemish styles.

During the period of Henry VII (1485–1509), iron chandeliers were brightly painted, sometimes draped with swags of rare rock crystal from Bavaria, and often studied with jewels and decorated with gold leaf. Both candelabra and chandeliers were made with removable branches, and while iron tripods for rushlights continued through from the Gothic period, many Spanish candlesticks served the rich in their manors and castles.

As the Fifteenth Century saw a change of interior decorating to the Continental taste, chandeliers for domestic use became more general, and Renaissance designs from Italy were soon to be found among the English styles.

A hanging light was called a 'candyl-beme' or 'belle canstyke'; there was also the 'great belle' candlestick, the 'lowe' candlestick and the 'aulter' candlestick. All looking a trifle outmoded against the imported fittings of carved and poly-chromed wood, some lavishly endowed with female figures and cupids.

English recognition of the now influential French taste, and her eagerness to follow the new but misinterpreted designs coming by way of the Netherlands, had already established the Renaissance by the time of Henry Tudor's death.

RENAISSANCE – TUDOR

The date of Henry VIII's accession to the throne (1509) has been conveniently accepted as the starting point of the English adoption of the Renaissance, although it had been earnestly encouraged by his father.

Indeed, Henry's subsequent break from the Roman Church completely blocked any direct Renaissance influence from Italy, and such detail as was made known to the educated few could only be conveyed by merchants and travellers crossing Europe with their remarkable tales of the excavations which were taking place in the hills around Rome.

Certainly the King had lavished some of his wealth on bringing craftsmen, glass blowers, artists, carvers and painters from the Netherlands, Italy and France to contribute their skills to the splendour of new styles in architecture, furnishings and lighting fittings.

For the poor, lighting devices had changed little since primitive times. Saxon dishes continued in service and the grease pan was augmented by rush lights and clay hand-lamps. Lighting fittings were expensive and individually made to order by the smith or the armourer, and for those who lived in cottages and small houses, the wooden candlebeam, or the iron wheel, or the simple table pricket, was their greatest pretension.

The well-to-do had candlesticks of silver

42   *Tudor chandelier, c.1509.*

hoop held plain candle sockets and drip pans (Plate 42).

An iron wall sconce of the Sixteenth Century has a vertical backplate surmounted by a crudely shaped *fleur-de-lis*. The candle arms project forward and hold short shafts supporting shallow pans and plain sockets.

A candlestick of later date shows a similar pan and socket mounted across the diameter of an open circle wrought on to a central shaft, and mounted on four domed feet. The centre of the circle has scrollwork springing from the main stem which projects beyond the edge of the circle to a finial. A wall sconce of about 1515 bears identical pans and sockets mounted on a tall backplate with an open scrollwork of

or pewter, and burned candles made of a mixture of wax and tallow with cotton wicks. A chandelier or lantern hung in the entrance, wall sconces provided light in the bed chamber and the principal rooms, and these had to be augmented by candlesticks. And in palaces and great houses, where no expense was spared to furnish in fashionable style, large chandeliers were made of brass imported from Flanders and Germany, or were of wrought iron from the local forge.

A hanging chandelier would have been about thirty-six inches in diameter, made in the form of a double hoop of strap iron separated by decorative scrollwork and suspended from spiral-twisted rods hooked on to a ring attached to the ceiling hook. Posts around the circumference of the

43   *Renaissance sconce, c.1515.*

crude leaf form within its frame (Plate 43).

It should be noted that the shallow saucer-like pan and the plain socket is a general characteristic of English lighting fittings as compared with the deep cup of the Spanish pan of roughly the same period. The shallow pan is also to be noted on the Dutch chandeliers and most of the fittings of the near Continent, but there are exceptions where the deep cup had been used in Southern France and the shallow pan in Spain because it served the decorative purpose to better advantage, and there was a time during the Tudor period when the deep cup appeared on English fittings.

Henry died in 1547 and his successor, Edward VI, lived only until 1553, to be succeeded by Mary Tudor (1553–58) who married Philip of Spain. The significance of the period is that it encouraged trading relations with Spain, and that trade included the introduction of iron candelabra, chandeliers, and tripod standards bearing several tiers of candles, all of which were to augment the increasing splendour of the English interior.

This exchange of ideas led to the involvement of deep cup pans with English backplate and branches, but either sockets, prickets or cages were used to hold the candles as there seemed to be no particular rule governing their use as a design feature.

Glass lamps were introduced from Barcelona, and although some Venetian glassware was owned by wealthy subjects of the Crown, there is no evidence of glass chandeliers or candlesticks having been in use at that time. Glass lighting devices were in the form of small float lamps and were probably confined in their use to some quite small household task. Oil was rather messy and smokey, and since candlemaking was fairly widespread there was no need to adopt the use of oils and fats which were illuminants popular with the lower classes.

Nevertheless, as candles formed a major part of household expenditure they were not to be had by the handful or used without good reason, and were therefore rationed by the household controller according to need. Some members of the staff would be allowed something in the order of '1 candle and 20 candle ends', another would be awarded '1 thick candle and 10 candle ends'.

The Crusader was a popular figure of legendary fame among the Tudors of this period, and his image was often reproduced as ornamentation on candlesticks and chandeliers. One six-light chandelier of Continental origin has as its centre shaft a hexagonal dome supported on buttress-shaped pillars which rise from the body of the fitting. In the centre is a Crusader with shield and sword and dressed in full mail armour (Plate 44). Candle arms project around the body of the fitting, rising in shallow upward curves to plain pans and hexagonal sockets. A trefoil motif breaks the otherwise severe line of the arms, and the lower body tapers downwards to a ring finial. This design was being reproduced as late as 1930.

Candlesticks in the form of an heraldic beast or an armoured knight were not uncommon among those who could afford them, and less elaborate sticks followed the Flemish style of the Fifteenth Century, having a high circular foot from the centre of which rose the cylindrical stem holding

44   Crusader chandelier, Tudor.

the candle socket. The baluster stem remained in vogue throughout the period, and some candlesticks had a tall candle socket brazed to the centre of the drip pan.

Removing the candle ends from cage sockets was a simple enough task, but removal from the cylindrical all-metal socket could be difficult unless access was given to the candle end; and so the chandelier makers cut an aperture in the lower half of the socket so that a small spike could be inserted to release the melted wax. Until about 1550, the aperture was a horizontal slot which allowed the melting grease to run out into the drip pan. Later fittings were given a vertical aperture on each side of the socket, sometimes surmounted by a circular hole.

After the Queen died, Philip returned to Spain to encourage the Inquisition, and during that time a good deal of the silverware of Spanish *Plateresco* period (1500–50) reached England, together with emigrant silversmiths, an occasion which introduced further foreign influence into home-produced silverware.

Naturally, when we speak of influence and changes, we are referring only to the principal cities and towns, for marshes and unpenetrated wilds came close to the city gates of London and York, and the greater part of the population lived by the plough, rising at first light and working until dusk. They had no use, or money, for fancy chandeliers, and most families spent their entire lifetimes knowing only the feeble light of the grease pan and the smokey flare of the rushlight.

The Elizabethan period (1558–1603) opened with a simpler, more refined style of decoration and architecture, largely influenced by the work of the Spanish architect Herrera, and often expertly executed by English craftsmen. There were many variations to all imported wares when they were reproduced, and even the readily available Netherlands chandeliers were copied in English metal.

Brass was mainly imported in ingots from Germany and Flanders, as it had been for about three centuries. English brass-making was known about 1585 and was called 'yellow metal' or 'latten'. Latten was brass, but was the product of brass ingots beaten into shape and wrought together to form the finished article.

It is more probable that the chandeliers and candlesticks that enriched the Tudor homes were made of bronze, the heavy red-brown product of copper and tin – often misguidedly called brass.

Silver and silver-gilt became favourite metals for the fashion-followers, and silver chandeliers were chased with arabesque designs in the Spanish manner.

A wall light (sconce) could be as simple as an oval reflector for the backplate, with scroll arms and shallow pans; or as elaborate as one with repoussé work reproducing popular motifs of the day.

One such sconce would be of case bronze in the form of a curtained canopy supported on double columns. A rayed motif was used as the backplate under the canopy and below this, a woman's bust. The canopy was surmounted by a classical turn, the whole being framed by formal scrollwork and foliage terminating in a shell. It is of interest, because all of these motifs are found prominently featured in the Georgian era over two hundred years later.

The typical Elizabethan 'Dutch' chandelier had the familiar baluster stem with a solid bronze ball at its base. The S-scroll arms had as their centre line a serpents head with mouth agape, holding firmly on to the upturning end of the scrolls which bore wide, shallow pans and simple cylindrical sockets (Plate 45).

But not all Flemish chandeliers of the Sixteenth Century were of this particular form, many had as their central supporting shaft one or more ecclesiastical figures; the Virgin and Child, or saints or priests, and they had slim scroll arms heavily decorated

45 *Netherlands chandelier, c.1600.*

with leaf-like reflectors. Most of these went into Churches and some are still in use.

Elizabethan latten candlesticks had a high domed foot with a spirally fluted, or horizontally corrugated shaft, which rose from a wide drip pan set on top of the domed foot.

Towards the end of the period, wrought iron became less elaborate as the blacksmiths were obliged to curtail the production of iron for domestic purposes because of the widespread destruction of forests and the resulting ban on opening new furnaces for their trade. This had the effect of turning the attention of craftsmen to other materials for luxuries such as domestic lighting fittings and door furniture.

With the exception of carved wood chandeliers, most lighting fittings were simple, much more simple than the attend- and furnishing and decoration. In stately homes, ceilings were elaborately carved and painted. Walls were hung with tapestry or were panelled in oak.

Stained glass sections held together by lead strips introduced colour into window glass. Here we must recall that Venetian glass was of the best quality so far produced, but even so, the best window glass was a patchy effect of chalky white or grey mist with small transparent areas; some glass being more transparent than others.

But since there was little of interest to be seen without, the affluent society chose to improve the effects from within, and delighted in beautiful coloured glass windows. This same coloured glass was used for lantern windows to please the eye and to attract attention, while the lesser residence made do with sections of scraped horn as window panes as well as for the windows in their lanterns.

STUART

The adventurous spirit of leading Eliza- bethans had inspired the educated and uneducated classes alike. It became fashion- able to sail the seas, to visit the Spanish coast and to head for Italy, that source of the wonderful new knowledge of ancient culture.

In the time of James Stuart (1603–25) (James I of England, James VI of Scotland) England and Scotland acquired a common bond for the first time, and the Seventeenth Century opened to a fresh outlook on fashion and furnishing.

Candlesticks of latten and pewter were fashioned after silver originals. Formal gadrooning appeared around the drip pans and around the foot. Chandeliers of solid silver were dressed with rock crystal from abroad, and the Dutch chandeliers, now popular and imported in quantity, were being copied by English chandelier makers. The variety of shapes used for the central stem, and the variation of design to be seen in shaping the arms, is evidence that each maker introduced his own preference and characteristic method of working. Some chandeliers are engraved with the maker's name, and there are experts who can determine the district of origin, or even the maker, by their knowledge of individual styles.

There were brass candlesticks with floral decoration, human figures, gargoyles and monsters, picked out in coloured enamel. Candlesticks typical of the early period were mounted on a trumpet foot rising to a stem, encircled, about half-way up, by a wide drip pan, often of the same diameter as the base. Candlesticks with ringed shafts and lipped sockets were common among the seventeenth-century designs, but the more elaborately decorated pieces were mostly of Continental origin. And leather workers made both hand and hanging lanterns, using scraped horn in the window space. These were still called lanthorns, and used one or two candles as the light source.

The Great Hall, the communal centre of every large household, would be served by several chandeliers suspended by chains or rope from the ceiling beams. Smaller hallways or entrance halls had one chan- delier or a lantern. The principal bed chambers, where ceiling height permitted, had a small chandelier of pewter or bronze, or the simple wooden cross-bar called a candlebeam.

For additional light there were wall sconces that could be transferred between rooms according to where the most light was needed. The candle pedestal, in wood or marble, began the long career that established its descendants as the 'candlestand' of the James II period, the *'torchère'* of the Georgians, the 'lamp stand' of the Victorians, and the 'espedistra stand' of the Edwardians; not to forget kindred family branches leading to the tripod-cum-table-cum-fire-screen, the tea table, and the modern standard lamp.

In this way the course of lighting was taken through to the time of Charles I (1625–49), during whose reign we note changes in glass-making abroad which were to affect the efficiency of lanterns and lighting glass the world over.

In 1633, in Bohemia, a revolutionary glass-making technique was evolved; it used a basic potash-lime composition which enabled the production of a perfectly clear and transparent glass, a glass which soon became known as 'Bohemian crystal'.

But from about 1640, the threat of civil war caused many of the wealthy families to withdraw their patronage from the arts and to take residence abroad. The ensuing era is therefore characterised by a simplicity of design and a deterioriation in workmanship, factors readily accelerated by Cromwell during the Commonwealth period (1649–60).

With theatres closed, the English Church disbanded and all forms of literary and pictorial art outlawed, events took place which set back the development of lighting fittings and furnishings a generation or

more, as the Roundheads plundered and the people concealed.

Much of the precious plate of the nobility and wealthy land owners was melted down to provide funds for the Crown. Treasures were removed or concealed, or smuggled out of the country, many of them never to be retrieved. Expensive chandeliers and candelabra were confiscated for their gold and silver to provide funds, or for their brass and iron to make armaments. Candlesticks, lanthorns and candelabrum of simple design were allowed to perform the majority of lighting tasks.

State buildings and reception rooms retained their simple Dutch style chandeliers, whether of foreign or English manufacture, their simplicity being a point of appeal to the Puritan outlook, and even they were treated with several layers of whitewash or paint to cover up the rich appearance of the metal.

Rush lights were in widespread use, and floor-standing rush holders were in the form of a vertical iron rod set in a heavy wooden base on the floor. Some rush holders had a weighted grip to hold the rushes as well as a socket to hold a candle.

Wrought iron, either blackened or whitewashed, was retained throughout the period, the deficiencies of which were more than adequately balanced by the succeeding events of the Restoration.

Upon the restoration of the sovereignty to the Stuart line through Charles II (1660–85), Samuel Pepys recalled '. . . all the world in a merry mood because of the King's coming'. Charles and his entourage, returning from a long exile on the Continent, brought with them extravagant and luxurious manners which John Evelyn described as 'the politer way of living'.

Continental fashions, manner and graces enriched the well travelled Court. Foreign carvers, chandelier makers, gilders and architects found their way into England as tutors or masters, and began to establish the Renaissance arts in their correct likeness and proportion.

In 1662, candles of wax began to replace those of tallow. Samuel Pepys, as Secretary to the Admiralty, began to use wax candles in his office in about 1663 to test the difference, and found considerable advantage since they did not need the frequent snuffing of the tallow candles, and the wax drippings remained adhered to the candle instead of spreading messily over the sconce and on to the floor or table.

The full impact of the new ideals was disastrously interrupted by the Plague of 1665 and the Great Fire of 1666 which destroyed some 13,000 timber-framed houses and their contents. Thus a good deal more of what might have come down to us through history had perished, and as the ranks of skilled craftsmen had been greatly depleted by death there was hardly anyone capable of restoring English crafts when the affliction had abated. However, it is remarkable how soon after the event that life was re-set on its previous course, with even greater enthusiasm and determination to re-build for the future.

This was the time of Grinling Gibbons (1648–1721), the great wood-carver who carved into woodwork delicately formed bunches of fruit, foliage, scrolls, cherubs, shells and dolphins, all of which appeared in the beautiful wall sconces made by him and his apprentices. The Classic Orders of architecture, accurately introduced earlier by Inigo Jones, were expertly executed by Christopher Wren in the next generation, for he was only twenty-two when Inigo Jones died.

Silver wall brackets were made with the crown surmounting a polished backplate, and around the edges were cherubs' heads and foliage (Plate 46). Sometimes the crown was replaced by a basket of fruit, and sometimes the cherubs were replaced by the male and female torso bordering the backplate with their lower limbs encased in foliage.

The familiar Dutch style chandelier was produced more frequently in silver, and was showing a distinct slimming of line and delicacy of workmanship. The begin-

46 *Silver sconce with cherubs, c.1680.*

ning of the S-scroll arm lost the serpent head of the Elizabethan model and started instead with a series of small pointed projections which appear to have overshot the curve of the arm – the forerunner of applied leafwork.

There was a vogue for placing polished discs at candle height to assist reflection of light. Occasionally other shapes, such as shields, birds or human figures were used by way of variation. Chandeliers from Germany, Russia and Poland were often surmounted by an eagle or a phoenix. Ringed candlesticks were now common property among the lower classes, while the middle classes enjoyed the use of candlesticks of latten, pewter and brass.

Candlesticks of moulded and blown glass became increasingly popular, and there were some chandeliers and wall sconces with demountable branches, which enabled a retiring member of the household to remove a candle branch, light his way to the bedchamber and fit the branch into the wall sconce or bedpost socket while preparing for bed. At daybreak, a servant would visit the bedchambers and return all the branches to the main chandeliers from whence they came.

The changing form of the chandelier becomes evident in the new designs in silver. Typical of the period is the Haddon Hall chandelier (c.1660), with its fine S-scroll arms fitted around the circumference of an open-work body sphere which terminates the slim baluster stem. Wall sconces to match have one, two or several branches springing from a backplate of the same open-work pattern (Plate 47).

It is significant because it shows for the first time how designs were beginning to

47   *Haddon Hall chandelier, c.1660.*

break from the inevitable Dutch style. The basic form is still there in the large body sphere and the baluster shaft, only this time the sphere is a lightly made basket of delicate scrollwork, and the shaft has been scaled down to more slender proportions. The arms are still of S-scroll shape, but are of slim tubular metal, more shallow than their predecessors and mounted directly on to the body instead of above it. The candle sockets are of shallow urn shape, and the drip pans are shallow saucers which are typical of most English lighting fittings.

Another traditionally silver chandelier is that which was originally designed for Knole House, and which is generally known as 'the silver Knole'. Cast with plain square-section scroll arms, the body comprises a delicately shaped baluster shaft rising from the main body. This body is finely chased in arabesque patterns, and is terminated in a large finial pineapple or pine cone.

The arms, springing from the body, are

48   *Knole House chandelier, c.1670.*

plain and vigorous; that section attached
to the body being an inverted 'C' which
carries a reversed 'C' up to the drip pans.
The pans are wide shallow saucers, chased
on the underside and bearing tall urn-shaped
sockets for the candles. Some models
were made with the head and shoulders of
cupids merging into formal pedestals, a
number of these being mounted so as to
encircle the shaft (Plate 48).

The Knole chandelier is dated c.1670,
and represents a complete break from those
designs which had for so long dominated
the best lighting fittings in England. It does,
however, bear a strong resemblance to
certain designs of Mazarin chandeliers of
c.1650, during the time of Louis XIV,
repeating the general silhouette and in
particular the use of cherubs around the
upper shaft. Both fittings are reproduced
to this day as electroliers (Plate 49).

Crystal chandeliers from France and
Bohemia were introduced into the domestic
scene, and although glass fittings continued

to be a rare possession there was ample
opportunities for improvement in their
manufacture, and there is mention of a
crystal chandelier in Whitehall as early as
1667.

The Bohemian glass works were now
producing a clearly transparent glass,
which they used mainly for stemware and
bowls. As a result, the Venetian glass
began to lose its attraction, and we find
less of it from about this time. Instead,
horse caravans, travelling from Bohemia
throughout Europe in the 1670s were
eagerly awaited.

Unless miniature samples were carried,
chandeliers and candlesticks were not
among the samples, but no doubt there were
drawings to show the designs which were
obtainable to special order.

49   *Mazarin chandelier, (English).*

In 1673 the London Glass Sellers' Company engaged with George Ravenscroft to manufacture glass according to his own formula, which later included a quantity of oxide of lead which, it was claimed, overcame the defects of previous formulae. Success matured during the next reign, but the occasion is important to the student who may be interested in the date of imported glass from Bohemia, and to note the introduction of lead crystal for the first time into English-made glass.

The use of improved wax candles reduced the need for large drip pans, and by 1690 the drip pan had been replaced by a rim around the socket. Some models had a vertical slit in the column fitted with a sliding lever for the removal of candle ends.

Candle snuffers had been introduced during Tudor times for the explicit task of trimming the thick wick as it burned leaving an increasing tail of charred material, and they too were liable to changes in design and shape, but basically snuffers are like scissors which bear a metal box on one blade to receive the charred snuff. During the reign of Charles II, snuffers became more delicate and more elaborate; sometimes housed in a tray made exactly to the shape of the snuffers and sometimes housed in an upright stand with a vertical socket to contain the snuffers. Some snuffer stands held additional implements such as a conical extinguisher (also at times referred to as a snuffer) and a spike for removing the candle from the socket.

Further down the social scale the furniture of a century ago was still in use and continuing to circulate from one generation to the next with few additions. Here they still burned open-flame oil lamps made of latten or iron, although a good many households enjoyed the slightly more sophisticated crusie, which seems to have been brought from Scotland with the Stuart monarchy. The open crusie was oval shaped, pinched to a wick channel at one end, and slightly flattened at the other so as to attach firmly to a carrying handle. Later models were fitted with a hinged lid, and by the end of the century further refinement was added by supporting a second pan below the first so that the drips from the wick could be caught and retained for further use.

Whale oil represented a relatively inexpensive form of illuminant and was burned in open pans and glass lamps, but it was far from popular because of its smell.

Crusies, pan lamps, rushlight holders and brass chandeliers formed the essentials of the American Colonial homes which now flourished in the far-off lands, and which, during the reign of James II (1685–88), became augmented by Continental brass chandeliers and candlesticks.

When William and Mary consented to become joint sovereigns over England (1689–1702), the Dutch influence was revived and even increased as skilled marquetry workers, cabinet makers and wood carvers followed their king to his new country. What the king's followers might have thought of English ways does not seem to have been recorded, but Mary, a woman of gentle nature, was astonished at the coarseness of the Stuart Court, notwithstanding its Continental background.

Although the Dutch influence was strong,

it was the French architect Daniel Marot, as Minister of Works, who imparted even more style to English design, in particular for the fashion of having elaborately carved wooden chandeliers in heavy Baroque style, often with the formal scroll overlaid with acanthus; a feature which introduced a more delicate touch to the strictly formal lines of the early period.

Crystal chandeliers of Bohemian, French and English make were in limited use, many of them being modelled on the familiar baluster-and-ball construction of their metal contemporaries. There were no swags of crystal buttons or tall spires such as glorified the glass chandeliers of the next century; they were plainly made and un-faceted, with scroll arms and large pans.

On wall sconces there was an extensive use of 'Boyes and Crownes', a motif comprising cherubs on either side of the Royal Crown surmounting a polished backplate or mirror, a design handed down from the previous period. Sometimes, just the cherubs heads were used, after the style of Grinling Gibbons, and frequently the crown was replaced by either a flaming crest or a motif of naturalistic fruit. One such bracket made by John Rand of London shows a highly decorated backplate with a central convex reflecting plate surrounded by gadrooning (Plate 50).

In 1697, the Britannia Standard came into force and remained until 1720. This compelled silversmiths to make their wares only from a mixture of 958 parts of silver to 42 of copper, thus providing a more pure metal than had previously been used. In consequence of the softer working surfaces decoration was kept simple, and broader techniques were used when elaborate decoration was needed, as is evident in the sconces of cherubs and garlands by John Rand.

Candlesticks were made with a polygonal stem and base; also with a simple baluster stem set on a square base, with the corners cut off, set back and rounded. The fittings of the period are noted for their excellent proportion and delicate appearance, and Britannia Standard pieces are collectors items which thread their way through the reigns of William and Mary, Queen Anne and George I.

In an obscure background of experiment, the use of the gas given off by coal had already been recognised as a possible source of light and heat. Most primitive of these was the coal kettle, a metal pot with a lid, a spout and a carrying handle. Burning coals were packed into the pot, and when

50   *Silver sconce, 1703.*

gas was emitted from the spout it could be ignited to provide a bright unsteady flame.

Dean Clayton of Kildare experimented with gas for lighting purposes as early as 1688, but did not reveal his work until 1732. Details of isolated areas were scarce indeed in those days of slow travel and little exploration, otherwise the West might have learned that in some parts of China gas was being obtained from beds of rock-salt at a depth of about 1,500 feet. This was brought to the surface and conveyed in bamboo tubes, being used on the one hand for the evaporation of brine, and on the other hand as a source of artificial light. They also experimented with the idea of filling skin bags with this natural gas, and igniting it as it escaped from a small hole made in the side of the bag, but this method does not seem to have been widely used.

During the reign of Queen Anne (1702–14), when furniture took another turn of design, lighting fittings changed also, not because of the change of monarch, but purely in the course of the evolution of design.

Glass candlesticks changed their style according to the amount of skill developed in their manufacture. For example, in 1695 they were made in baluster form with a trumpet foot. In 1700, the domed foot appeared surmounted by a sphere which supported the stem and candle socket. About 1715, the stem had become embellished with tings (blobs of decorated glass applied to the main piece) and knops (bulged knops in the stem), and the foot was ribbed and domed.

Candelabra, or branched candlesticks, were first made in England in silver in about 1660, but either little has survived or not very many were made, since the most prolific era seems to be the Eighteenth Century, and silver candlesticks before 1600 are not known.

However, there is a clear succession of design which marks the passing years. The trumpet foot and cylindrical stem of the 1650s had its wide circular drip pan set low just above the foot, and there was a pronounced rim around the candle socket.

A square appearance came in the 1660s, with a square foot, stepped up towards a tall square, fluted column. Just above the foot, a square platform like a drip pan bore an acanthus motif, and a wide lip surrounded the socket.

The columnar candlestick, which appeared during the reign of Charles II, was in the classical form of a Roman Doric column, which remained popular into modern times.

By the 1690s, the wide pan and fluted column began to diminish in popularity in favour of the plain baluster stick, and then there came a general slimming and simplifying of most silverware.

By the early 1700s the drip pan had disappeared, leaving a plain socket tapering towards a baluster knop on the stem which in turn merged into a skirted flair just above the wide foot. Most of these were cast and came in various shapes, square, round, octagonal and hexagonal, the stem rising directly from the centre of the foot, or recessed in a slight dish-shaped centre; and within these limits silversmiths achieved some of the most tasteful work of the Queen Anne – Early Georgian period.

Glass chandeliers were produced in limited numbers and were individually made to order. They were mainly of plain baluster form with solid glass S-shaped arms and plain drip pans. As yet there were no pendants for draping around the pans or for making swags to drape between them. The glass remained quite plain, but since it was usually of the brilliant English lead crystal, the appearance continued to excite admiration wherever they were seen.

Altogether the most noticeable feature of fittings and furniture was the delicately feminine treatment in the restrained use of applied leafwork, feathers, scrolls and in the pronounced use of the shell as a motif. Transitional sconces of the 1700–1704 vintage feature all of these embellishments, and show the introduction of milled or rope edging to the pans, and a decorative knop in the centre of the arms.

The hexagonal shaft and body, which carried through to Georgian times, was also a familiar design in Queen Anne fittings. The hexagonal section S-scroll arm had a well proportioned knop in the centre of the curve. Drip pans were milled around the edge and gadrooned on the underside. Sockets were tubular and slim to compliment the taller, slimmer candles of the day.

Designs were largely influenced by the Huguenots with their love of acanthus, scrolls and gadrooning, but even their tendency to over-elaborate fell into line with the requirements of current fashion, and as, towards the end of the reign, the simpler shape of candlesticks was followed by simpler chandelier design, so we find an interesting example in which simplicity and decorative flair are blended well together.

51   Silver chandelier, c.1705.

This model breaks entirely from the conventional ball and urn shapes of previous chandeliers, ignores hexagonals and octagonals, and is based instead on the central body being given the appearance of two large silver cymbals having been mounted face inwards on either side of a deep, milled band. The top section tapers into a simple central shaft terminating in a suspension ring. The lower section flares downwards to a gadrooned cover from which depends a large acorn.

The band which unites the two sections of the body is deeply milled, and set around it at regular intervals are the candle arms, which are cast in a shallow S-curve resembling a door knocker, and being partly overlaid with leaf-work. The up-curving end of the scroll bears a gadrooned cup on which rests a flat, milled edge pan, and the candle socket is tall and vase-shaped (Plate 51).

Large chandeliers of carved wood, either in its natural unpolished state or painted, were often mounted with three or four tiers of candles, and hung from chains covered with silk cords and coloured tassels.

Attention was also being paid to lighting the streets. Standard lanterns were mounted at intervals along the main thoroughfares or at street corners. Bracket lanterns, tended by the watchman, shed their rays from the shop fronts. Flares and wall cressets burned tarred rope along the waterfront, and at turnpike gates the fire basket battled valiantly with the night winds; in all, a strong contrast with the fashionable interior of the period.

When Anne died, the Stuart line came to an end, and made way for an even more dramatic and spectacular era of history.

GEORGIAN

George of Hanover, unable to speak English and unwilling to involve himself too heavily with English customs, came to the throne as George I (1714–27) to commence the great Georgian era which was to include four kings, a romantically notorious regency, and 116 years of decorative magnificence produced by some of the greatest architects and designers of all time.

As it happened, the styles of the Queen Anne period merged easily with the few innovations of her successor, but the plain fashions of this early period were destined to unfold into exciting new ideas of style and décor.

The heavy formal scrolls and framework of the Baroque had already experienced a more delicate treatment, and now appeared with oak or acanthus leaves for decoration, with gadrooning or rope effect on the pans, base plate and candle sockets. Chandeliers began to increase in size with arms of square-section, carved leafwork and heavily ornamented shafts.

The Britannia Standard continued to keep silverware relatively simple, although the more adventurous workers were now introducing more decoration than in previous work.

It was not until the latter years of the reign that fittings came under the belated influence of those designs popular during the long reign of Louis XIV of France (1643–1715), and subsequently promoted by the French craftsmen at work in England.

European walnut was now in short supply due to the heavy demands of the past. British timber importers were unable to obtain walnut from France, their chief source of supply; and when in 1720 the French government banned its export it became necessary to use Virginian walnut as a substitute.

Mahogany also made its appearance, and being a hard wood could be finished without needing extravagant carving to embellish the surface. Mahogany chandeliers and attendant lighting pieces were plain with little carving and with bevelled edges up to about 1730.

The period did bring its attendant deceptions. It so happened that the Virginian dark walnut closely resembled mahogany, and once it had been fashioned and stained the deep red popular at that time, hardly anyone could detect the difference. Except that in the course of time the Virginian walnut gave way to the task of battling with the atmosphere and candle smoke, while the hardy mahogany survived with an untarnished reputation.

For the first time, with the exception of Inigo Jones and Christopher Wren, the names of the architects, furniture makers and cabinet makers, actually became as prominent as that of the monarch during whose reign they worked.

From about 1720, the originality and versatility of William Kent (1685–1748) established the popular taste for classic architecture, with furnishings to match, and, for good measure, extensive landscaping of the surrounding countryside. His partnership with the second Earl of Burlington established the Palladian style in England and to the massive and beautifully executed chandeliers of the reign of George II (1727–60).

Wood was used principally because it could more easily be used to imitate the mood of the furniture. Chandeliers, in gilded walnut or mahogany, had a heavily carved centre shaft fitted to a deep body, from which sprang the scroll arms to hold the candle pans. Chippendale favoured a break from the formal scrolls and hexagonals of some of his contemporaries, and made chandeliers whose arms were of gentle up-curving C-scrolls with carved floral decoration. These radiated from a deep circular body which flared upwards into the shaft made like a finely proportioned vase with floral handles.

Brackets supported on heavy Baroque scrolls were provided on the walls, not for the display of marble busts as is sometimes supposed, but for the placing of candelabra should extra light be needed.

There was also the great *torchère,* often a pedestal formed by the human figure in wood, bearing a tray or architectural

52   *Chandelier for the Czar of Russia.*

pediment on its head. These too were for candelabrum.

The Frenchman, Paul de Lamerie, the greatest silversmith since Cellini, had been brought up in England since 1691; he was pupil of Peter Platel of Pall Mall, and emerged in 1712 as a silversmith in his own right, with an address in Windmill Street, London.

His early work in candlesticks was done during the time of the Britannia Standard and was in the more simple forms, but long after other workers had returned to sterling silver after 1720, he continued to work in the finer silver for more than a decade, leaving many beautiful pieces for the delight of connoiseurs the world over.

One of his most famous chandeliers was made for the Czar of Russia, and bore sixteen lights in two tiers, the shaft surmounted by a crown, and the reverse scroll of each arm bearing a bearded face whose lower jaw merged with the second scroll (Plate 52).

Between 1730 and 1740, the first shaping appeared on the pans (or sconces) of glass chandeliers in the form of scalloping or petals. From 1760, decoration was cut into the glass as flat diamond facets and vertical fluting.

Crystal buttons in swags and drapes hung between the pans and from the top of the stem, throwing shimmering pin-points of candlelight across the room to reflect again and again in the tall pier mirrors between the windows. The 'dressed' chandelier was making its entrance in Georgian England.

Throughout such a long era no style remained exactly in the form in which it had begun, and no craftsman worked in the same style and with the same designs throughout his career. And even while the Palladian school built its fine villas and its monumental furniture, the uniformity of the Baroque gave way to the asymmetric silhouette of the rococo style from France.

This began near the end of the reign of George I in about 1725, occupied the thoughts of designers during the whole of the reign of George II (1727–60) and faded from popularity in 1763 during the reign of George III (1760–1820). Moreover, the form of rococo is to be seen in varying degrees of emphasis through to the 1860s, but it is the rococo as introduced by Paul de Lamerie in silver and by Chippendale in furniture that appeals to the hard core of 'purists' of rococo art in England.

In the form of the original *rocaille* ornamentation that had developed in France during the Regency of Louis XV (1715–23), it consisted of naturalistic floral curves, rockery with flowing water and shell forms, all blended into the shape of some functional article such as mirror frame, dinner plate, candlestick or chandelier. Later rococo decoration is more restricted to foliage and swirling scrolls overlaid with acanthus leaf, or formed of oak leaves with acorns.

53   Rococo candlestick, c.1760.

Candlesticks of the period show a positive break from symmetrical proportions as the swirling leafwork forms the foot, stem and candle socket; even so, the English rococo is generally more restrained than the French (Plate 53). Chandeliers and wall sconces followed *en suite,* copying the finest Louis designs in gold, silver and bronze, fincly cast and then chiselled into the intricate designs which governed the style.

Other interesting changes were also taking place, for example, the typical sweetmeat stand of the 1750s had a central vase-shaped stem mounted on a square base. Radiating from the mouth of the vase were several scroll arms bearing the cut glass dishes for the sweetmeats. Swags of crystal drops were suspended between the dishes, the dishes themselves being hung with almond-shaped drops cut from rock crystal. With a little modification, in which candle cups were fitted inside the dishes, the sweetmeat stand became a beautiful candelabrum, and there were also exquisite centre pieces which were both sweetmeat stands and candelabrum combined.

All the earlier crystals were in almond or pear-drop shapes, and the swags were composed of double-sided cut-glass buttons joined together with gold wire. Glass lighting fittings were made with the same theme of decoration, buttons, drops and swags being suspended in profusion from every possible position.

When the spectacular flow of the rococo was losing favour in France, it was arrested in England by the formal classical styling introduced by Robert Adam (1728–92), who, after studying in Italy from 1754 to 1759, now dictated the forming of the Classical Revival in England, a parallel to be found in France in the hands of Percier and Fontaine in *le style Louis Seize.*

Superb lighting fittings were designed to compliment the decorations and architecture of the rooms, and Adam is as much noted for his chandeliers and lamps as for his furniture.

Bronze, silver, gold, glass and wood were used extensively to match the fine furnishings, while pewter or zinc, or tin or lead, sufficed when expense had to be considered. Brass accounted for a high proportion of candlesticks used by the middle classes, but iron, except for street furniture as balconies, railings, lamp standards or torch extinguishers, was hardly used. But neither iron or wood escaped Adam's attention when required to serve his purpose, and during the 1780s he designed candlesticks and lamp stands in both materials.

Carved wood, gilded and sometimes overlaid with ormolu mounts produced by Matthew Boulton in Birmingham, was used for wall lights and large chandeliers. A wooden bracket of the period is elaborately carved and gilded, being composed of a gadrooned urn supported on a sunburst plinth on a tapering fluted column. The urn is ringed with laurel leaves and overflows with roses and fuchsias. Four candle arms curve outwards and downwards ending in jar-shaped sockets.

A bracket in ormolu is composed of a tall fluted column surmounted by a laurel-draped urn. Three deeply curved arms are overlaid with leaf-work and support decorated pans and sockets. The central arm arises from between the horns of a ram's head.

Glass chandeliers and candelabra were tall, elegant and delicately fashioned, with spires, almond drops, tear drops and swags of crystal buttons to adorn their curving arms and tall stems.

The candlestick now underwent its first major change for almost a century, with the disappearance of the simple fluted column in favour of a full Corinthian column with the candle socket fitted into its capital. There was a fashionable model with a square base from which arose a tapering square-section stem terminating in a vase-shaped socket. In the 1740s these were of plain case brass and were made elaborate with chased detail in the latter years of their production.

About 1750, a process was evolved in Sheffield which was called silver plating, and which afterwards became the famous Sheffield Plate. The process involved layers of silver and copper rolled into sheets and fused together, being moulded with all the embossing and decoration of the more expensive solid silverware. Old Sheffield Plate, also called copper plate, which has been well polished over the years shows the red tint of the copper appearing through the silver overlay, and this effect is considered to be one of the attractions of old pieces.

Nearly all of the Sheffield Plate candlesticks between 1760 and 1840 are in fashionable rococo ornament or in the classical style of Adam, and most candlesticks made between 1765 and 1840 were of Sheffield Plate. There is one variant which occurs between 1830–40 which

involved the use of nickel and brass (nickel-silver) in order to assist in maintaining a good white colour during wear. The Sheffield Plate process continued to be popular until the 1840s when a method of electroplating was found to be cheaper and more in sympathy with the newly developing Industrial Age.

54   *Adam candlestick, c.1775.*

Adam candlesticks of 1775 have a tapering column and square foot, and bear mouldings typical of the period. Around the candle socket are swags of leaves. In the top of each panel in the column is a wreathed goat's head surrounded by garlands. Beading divides the four sections of the square base, and

55 *Crystal* girandole, *c.1780.*

each section is embossed with an urn (Plate 54).

The candlestick business at Sheffield deteriorated as silversmiths began to use sheet silver to made candlestick components, soldering the parts together to make the whole article. The hollow centres which resulted from this method were filled with resin to give the impression of weight.

In the 1780s we find a further modification to the earlier sweetmeat dish, which, having been redesigned as the first of the crystal candelabra, was now taken further in the course of its evolution.

A tall spire, centrally placed and fitted into the vase-like mouth of the shaft, upheld a glass dome from which depended cut-glass lustres and swags. The same plan repeated in the drip pans gave the whole assembly the appearance of a fairground roundabout, especially as all the pans as well as the dome were free to revolve when touched. Consequently we find the description 'roundabout candlestick' or 'girandole' entering into the jargon of the day (Plate 55).

The most expensive chandeliers were of rock crystal, imported and cut in England by the famous glass houses. Less expensive, but of great beauty, were the English lead crystal fittings, made, cut and assembled on their home ground (Plate 56). Bohemian potassium crystal chandeliers followed in line of popularity, and were gradually taking on different forms under the influence of the changing designs in France.

All chandeliers were heavily draped with crystal, and it was the skilful pastime of intelligent ladies to re-dress the swags and

56   Crystal chandelier, c.1785/8.

pendants in different arrangements. If any of the components were broken during re-arrangement or cleaning, the parts were sent to the glassworks for replacement.

When a new shape of drop was introduced, sufficient quantities would be ordered to enable existing chandeliers to be re-dressed in fashionable taste. One may, therefore, come across an original fitting dressed out with crystal festoons and pendants of a later period, or an English chandelier dressed with French drops.

English glass would have enjoyed even wider acclaim had not the government imposed heavy excise taxes on clear crystal, and when in 1780 the tax was doubled, the exodus of English glassmakers and cutters to Ireland (where no such tax

existed) seriously reduced the labour force necessary to maintain the industry at home. Raw materials were produced from England, manufactured in Ireland and imported into England as a finished product, more often than not to be regarded as an entirely English product in later days.

The famous Cork and Waterford glass factories were established in 1783, and the Mulvaney factory at Dublin in 1785, all of which produced glass that became world famous within the decade. In England, the most dominant manufacturer of crystal chandeliers of the second half of the century was William Parker of Fleet Street, who was responsible for making the lovely chandeliers in the Assembly Room at Bath.

More luxurious than the single candle-sticks were the ornamental girandoles, which were hung with crystal pendants and festoons. Mostly they were mounted on decorative ormolu or silver bases, and many of the most exquisite designs were four feet tall, mounted on bases fashioned in the now famous Wedgwood jasperware, with cameo pictures against a background of blue or pale green.

In 1788, the plain tubular scroll arms, which had so far been in general use on glass lighting fittings, gave way to arms which were cut with a series of shallow gouges to provide extra facets for reflecting the light – an event which provides the lighting historian with another clue as to the probable date of a design. In the same way we may later note that the 'icicle' crystal was introduced during the early 1800s, and that it formed an important feature during the following period.

One must appreciate the overall plan of interior decoration which included these fine chandeliers and companion pieces. Throughout the changing of time, the changing of fashion affected the entire way of living for those whose wealth and position allowed them the luxury of whims and fancies.

Designers laid down a complete scheme for furnishing and decoration in which ornaments, paintings, ceilings, chairs and chandeliers became integral with the whole design. For example, under the guidance of Robert Adam, and in the workshops of Chippendale, Hepplewhite, Cobb and Vile, furniture was changed in appearance with the changing trends of current thinking. The straight tubular or square tapering leg had replaced the cabriole shape of the previous era. There were now massive sideboard-tables, flanked by urns on pedestals and including wine coolers., Decorations included such classical motifs as rams' heads, honeysuckle, roundels, medallions, fluting, sunrays, urns, ewers, swags, bunches of fruit, floral arrangements and the ancient key pattern.

Georgian England was predominently under the spell of candlelight, and even the relatively efficient oil-burning lamps from abroad were not acceptable in fashionable circles until re-designed by Adam. Not that the efficiency of the new lamps was at fault. Aimé Argand, a Swiss chemist who had been working in France during the period 1782–84, had exhibited his improved design for a lamp at the Academy of Science, and during his visit to England patented his design in 1784, having the first lamp made in the same year by Boulton & Co.

In this model, the wick was formed into a cylinder around a central tube to allow air to pass through the wick and increase its rate of burning, an effect accelerated by the inclusion of a glass chimney which created another current of air on the outside of the wick. The heavy colza oil was fed down from an oil font mounted above the level of the burner, a feature which is used to identify Argand lamps throughout the periods, although, it is fair to say that there were some improvements in design, oil delivery or the appearance of the metal shade which was held in place over the top of the chimney to direct the light downwards.

Such lamps were expensive, and probably not so efficient as we generally believe, but they nevertheless represented the most brilliant and steady source of light so far produced by artificial means, although they were quite beyond the means of the population at large.

It is not difficult to imagine the work involved in maintaining the domestic lighting at the higher levels of society. Oil lamps had to be trimmed, recharged with oil and have their smoke-blackened chimneys cleaned at intervals during the day and evening. Some lamps, in passages, street door lantern cases, and on stairways, were burned throughout the night.

Candles had to be replaced, trimmed and straightened. The usable candle ends were returned to the servants' quarters, melted together and moulded with fresh wicks into full-sized candles for use below stairs. The better candles were stored in candle boxes placed at convenient points about the house. Candle-cups and drip-pans on candlesticks and chandeliers had to be cleared of wax and polished. Smoke-bells above lamps and candles were cleaned, lantern glass washed, and tapers and tinder boxes replenished.

These tasks, together with others like replenishing coal for the fires, topping-up the water kettles and wash-stand jugs, and cleaning the rooms, became almost perpetual in the larger residence, and so they were distributed among staff especially employed for the purpose. Thus we find the 'coalman' to stoke the fires, the 'waterman' to renew the water, the 'cleaners' to clean the house, and the 'lamp and candle man' to maintain the lighting arrangements. These, in addition to the rest of the domestic staff. The small room in which all the impedimenta for this task was kept, was called the 'lamp and candle room'.

Even as the fashion for strictly Adam-designed rooms began to wane in favour of recently introduced French décor, a small but important event in the history of lighting by gas went almost unnoted.

In Whitehaven, Cumberland, Mr. Spedding, a coal mine manager, had successfully lit a group of offices, using coal gas as the medium. In 1765 he had put forward a proposal for the installation of street lighting by gas, but this was rejected by sceptical superiors. In 1792, the engineer, Richard Murdock, installed gas lighting in his home and business offices at Redruth, Cornwall; following up his experiment some years later by lighting the offices of Boulton and Watts in Birmingham.

But the most positive attempt to gain public interest was made by Frederick Albert Winsor of Moravia, who took up residence in Green Street just off Grosvenor Square. His object was to introduce gas lighting to those in a position to pursue its possibilities as a general lighting medium.

In 1803 and 1804 he publically exhibited his gas lighting scheme at the Lyceum Theatre, London, displaying various types of burner and explaining the production and distribution of domestic gas, the subject being explained via an interpreter reading from Winsor's notes while Winsor himself demonstrated the exhibits.

It was shown that the inflammable coal gas could be passed into narrow pipes, regulated by a tap and allowed to escape through a small hole described as the burner, where it could be ignited by a lighted taper. The light from it was brighter than that from candles, and additionally gave off a valuable radiation of heat.

Winsor's belief in the future of lighting by gas was firmly rooted in an idea that the installation of individual gas-making plants was expensive and inefficient, and that central gas works should be built for the storage and large-scale distribution of the gas to houses and business premises.

While his efforts to interest the public and financial backers in his project were not received with much interest by the majority, there were those who could foresee a future for this curious invention, and in 1809 gas street lighting was installed at Carlton House Terrace, a spirited move which brought hundreds of sight-seers to stare at the lamps which needed no wick and no oil.

The pioneer attempt at gas lighting was successful enough to urge Winsor to greater efforts, and in 1810 he promoted a company with the illustrious title of 'The Patriotic Imperial and National Light and Heat Company', which, in 1812 became the long-lived 'Gas, Light and Coke Company'.

Indoors, early burners were used without any protection for the flame, and the first shades for gas fittings were the glass candle shades from chandeliers and candlesticks. But shades were the exception rather than the rule, since most people considered gas lighting as nothing but a novelty, and a highly dangerous one at that.

However, proof of the tenacity of the pioneer gas companies is adequately expressed in records which show that by 1820, street gas lighting was so wide-spread that there was in the region of 40,000 street lamps in operation about that time, an observation which takes us just a step ahead of our story, for at the end of the reign gas caused little excitement, and the best quality crystal chandeliers continued to be the status symbol of the day, being in the same class as owning one's own Sedan chair, keeping black servants, or having just completed the Grand Tour.

THE REGENCY

Due to extreme ill health, George III was retired from his duties, and from 1811 to 1820, the Prince of Wales, as Prince Regent, headed the fashionable and extravagant Court, by which time the great architects of the previous era were dead; Robert Adam in 1792 and Sheraton in 1806, representing the end of the creative classical era.

It was now from the furnishings and decorations of Napoleon's Empire that the style of English Empire (or Regency as it was later re-named) arose, and a new exciting mode of living invaded the fashion-conscious social circles.

The change was not exactly sudden, as like most changes in fashion it had been materialising for some time, and even Adam had at one time followed the Egyptian vogue. From about 1800, the architecture and furnishing styles of Henry Holland had began to change the background of gracious living, the designs of the later period were produced by Thomas Hope and George Smith, as the leading English experts on Empire furnishings, and so by 1810 the Egyptian taste had been established by them and their contemporaries.

The period is widely misunderstood since it is often associated almost exclusively with furniture by Chippendale and Hepplewhite, and the chandeliers from the previous decade, but while the furniture of the now dead masters certainly continued in use throughout the Regency, an entirely different set of designs and motifs dominated the English Empire style.

The cast and finely finished forms of women in Hellenistic garments, putti, eagles, sphinxes, elephants bearing castles, Egyptian slaves, dolphins and negro figures were among the motifs in general use, all supported handsomely by decorative ormolu mounts.

The most ardent of the leaders in this developing style was a rich eccentric named Thomas Hope, of Deepdene in Surrey. He was undoubtedly a scholar in architecture, archaeology and interior design, for in 1807 he published an all embracing volume on interior decor entitled *Household Furniture and Interior Decoration,* in which he demonstrated his idea for a well regulated, museum-like décor which included both Greek and

Egyptian ornament and furnishing styles. But Hope designed for the wealthy, while John Smith, furniture draughtsman and upholsterer, followed in 1808 with his publication *Household Furniture* which, although it detailed elaborate designs, catered for the less wealthy and for those who had not fallen under the spell of Thomas Hopes ideals.

Chairs, couches and footstools, built upon Grecian scrolls, and table tops mounted on tripod feet or balanced firmly in the uplifted tails of a group of Dolphins characterised the new designs. The sabre-leg proved a popular and elegant shape for chair legs, and arm rests were frequently supported on the heads of mummified figures, or upon winged griffins, female sphinxes or muscular lions.

Mahogany was stained a vivid red and then polished by the French method of applying layers of shellac dissolved in spirit, a process which appeared in England in about 1815. Interiors were colourful, often in pastel shades, and were purposely designed towards a sunny and graceful impression, a condition which had been largely the concept of Robert Adam, and which continued to inspire the busy Brighton architect Charles Busby.

Crystal chandeliers underwent the most determined change of shape since their introduction. The S-scroll candles arms were mounted around the circumference of a decorated metal hoop, while inner hoops of diminishing sizes were mounted like an inverted pyramid, and hung with fringes of crystal icicle drops. Above the hoop was a tall tapering canopy composed of vertical strings of glass buttons; the

57 Regency 'balloon', c.1811.

whole fittings being suspended on silk-shrouded rope or chain.

Sometimes the top of the canopy, or pavilion as it was often called, terminated in an elaborate display of gilt palm leaves which spread outwards on to the ceiling. As an alternative, the rows of hanging icicle drops were replaced entirely by a large bag made up of glass buttons, which made the whole fitting look like a balloon turned upside down (Plate 57).

Some fittings consisted of a large diameter ormolu hoop fitted like a cartwheel to a centre shaft, with festoons of crystal diameter, and composed of 5000 separate pieces of glass.

The upper section of the body was capped by three hoops decreasing in size towards the top. From within the lower tier cascades of crystal buttons in strings descended gently outwards to terminate on the hoop which also bore the candle arms.

Each candle arm terminated in a glass sconce and socket and each sconce was surrounded by a fringe of icicle drops. From the main hoop, several smaller hoops, each closely hung with fringes of crystal drops, were suspended in decreasing diameter, until, finally, in descending geometry, the fringes came together at a central point at which hung a cut glass finial.

Such a chandelier, from Wroxton Abbey, Oxfordshire, is dated c.1810–20, and is displayed in the Victoria & Albert Museum (Plate 58).

Between 1815 and 1830 the cascade-and-waterfall design underwent two important changes. First, several of the lower inner tiers were removed and replaced by a shallow dish-shaped bag made up of strings of graduated crystal buttons, giving the effect of a crystal dish surrounded by fringes of icicle drops. Secondly, all the tiers were removed to be replaced by a large hanging basket of crystals, a design anticipated during the late 1780s, but not taken up as being fashionable until now.

There were similar chandeliers in which the candle branches were replaced by brackets for holding oil lamps, either held around the circumference of the hoop or concealed within the crystal canopy and bag. Candelabra for pier table and mantlepiece were elaborate with diamond-cut

58 Wroxton Abbey chandelier, 1810/20.

buttons draping from the top of the shaft down through the hoop and gathered upwards and outwards to the circumference of the hoop, the whole resembling the top of a pointed tent. C-scroll arms, typical of the period, were set around the hoop for the candles. Alternatively the candle sockets were set around the band itself so that there were no scroll arms.

The period 1800–1815 saw the development of cascade-and-waterfall designs which often reached monumental proportions, being ten feet high by five feet in patterns, and hung with slender lustre drops, sometimes in the clear crystal and often in the more expensive coloured glass which had become the fashionable thing to possess.

Although Robert Adam had designed some beautiful oil lamps, several types were imported from France which burned colza oil and which were not all that effective unless the oil font was made higher than the lamp reservoir, or, as an alternative, fitted with an internal clockwork mechanism that pumped the heavy oil to the wick-chamber. There were also lamps designed with a manual pumping system fitted into the metal oil font, so that as the flame showed signs of weakening, someone had only to press the plunger up and down several times in order to force fresh oil up to the wick.

The Argand burner, which introduced air into the centre of a cylindrical wick to encourage continuous burning and a brighter flame, had been growing in popularity since its invention by Aime Argand, whose business, Argand and Elgar of 37 Bruton Street, was rivalled only by that of J. Smethurst of 138, New Bond Street.

Argand died in 1803, but the principle of his air-burner remained the most revolutionary design of the period, appearing in several improved models such as the Astral lamp, the Carcel and the Moderator, the latter two versions have their oil font built into the body of the lamp. Both were pump-lamps with clockwork motors and winding keys which projected from the lamp, the key of the Carcel lamp being fitted to the base, and the key to the Moderator being terminated to its mechanism immediately below the burner.

Because of the fountain-feed principal of the Argand lamp, a large shadow was cast where the light-rays were obstructed by the font. To overcome this defect in design a lamp was so designed that the oil tank formed a hollow ring which also supported the dome-shaped glass shade. Oil was fed down through two or more tubes which held the ring to the main body of the lamp, thus gravity-feeding the Argand type burner. This was called the Sinumbra lamp.

The burner, tank and shade were supported as one unit by a decorated fluted column mounted on a circular base standing on a marble or wooden plinth. These lamps were also fitted with a patent wick-raiser, and a colourfully decorated glass shade.

Lamps were being made in quantity, chandeliers and candelabra were sold in shops which specialised in lighting fittings for the wealthy, and there were large

59 *Argand burner, Nineteenth Century.*

numbers of candlesticks with painted ground-glass shades. And the typical Argand lamp with its high oil font, projecting arms and air-wick system was probably the most widely manufactured lamp of them all (Plate 59). It appeared as a single hanging lamp, or as a chandelier with burners in place of candles (correctly known as a 'lampadier') or as a wall mounted lamp *en suite* with mantel-arm lamps for the mantelpiece.

Large candle lanterns were easily adapted for using oil lamps, and with the candle branches removed, the oil fitting could be mounted inside the lantern case, the increase of light output being almost unbelievable at that time.

As the single and double Argand burners became more common, lamp manufacturers incorporated them within the lantern framework instead of making the lanterns specifically for candles, and lamps of this kind were used in large houses up and down the country. An illustration, dated April 1821, shows the four hanging lanterns which lit the magnificent kitchen of the Royal Pavilion at Brighton, and each one is fitted with a double Argand burner.

But under the influence of the artistic and progressive Prince of Wales, it is not surprising that the latest developments in furnishing and lighting should have been incorporated in his luxurious seaside palace. A royal residence since 1787, and the centre of the Court for long periods during the Regency, the Pavilion was built and improved upon during one of the richest creative periods in history, and survives today as a standard reference of Regency art and a monument to the English Romantic Movement.

It is the place in which to study and understand the art of English Empire period, and to appreciate the inspired designs of Thomas Hope; a place in which to dwell and communicate with the past; to imagine, perhaps, the occasion of the 5th of November 1805 when news of the Battle of Trafalgar was brought to His Royal Highness at the Pavilion.

When the Prince of Wales planned to rebuild the original palace at the end of the Eighteenth Century there was a growing interest in the picturesque styles from the Orient, and the Chinese idiom adopted for the interior décor was carried to its elaborate yet exquisite completion by the celebrated architect John Nash between 1815 and 1821. The choice was popular and not entirely unexpected as the Oriental fashion had been in vogue long before this time, and almost every large residence had its Chinese room and its 'Chinese' Chippendale furniture.

Not every detail of the redecoration scheme was the personal inspiration of Nash; the Prince of Wales was the prime mover of the entire refurnishing project, and his association with Nash engaged also the skills and services of eminent decorators such as Robert Jones and Messrs Crace & Sons, the latter having designed the Chinese style candle lanterns which went into the corridor and elsewhere in the building.

The most up-to-date innovation, however, was not the fine furnishings or the pretty wallpapers, but the decision to introduce the newly acquired art of lighting by coal-gas, and this idea really added the final touch of opulance to the already exotic Pavilion.

The Pavilion grounds were the first areas around the royal residence to be lit by gas, and as this was such a successful venture, the decision was taken to proceed with lighting the interior by means of specially commissioned gasoliers in the principal rooms, a contract made possible by the building of a gas works by the Gas Light & Coke Co., at Black Rock.

In fact, the site at Black Rock was not within the boundaries of Brighton, but in the Parish of Rottingdean, to avoid the payment of a levy of 6d (pre-decimal) per ton on all coal brought into the town. This first gas works was established during 1818–19, and its supply of coal had to be landed from ships on to the beach, and then either hauled up the cliff or transported in carts through a tunnel leading from the shore.

The main lighting fittings in the Corridor, the Music Room and the Banqueting Room were made and installed by Messrs Perry & Co., of London, and not only were they a sheer fantasy of designing skill but also a triumph of manufacturing techniques, and were probably the greatest technical attraction of their day, just because they were gasoliers and derived their supply from the new gas works at Black Rock.

The importance of the installation and the interest which it had aroused within the Court circles lead naturally to the ceremony of turning on the gas and lighting the fittings for all to admire. This event took place in September 1818, and both His Royal Highness and John Nash were present for the occasion.

The gasoliers in both the Music Room and the Banqueting Room still have their gas pipes and burners in place, and if one studies the patterns on the glass panels when the fittings are illuminated from within one can see the silhouette of the old pipes in the form of a hoop suspended within the body of the fittings.

Gas burners were also built into the pedestal lamps which stand along the walls on either side of the Banqueting Room. These were designed about 1820 by Robert Jones, and are of blue Spode porcelain, ormolu and wood, with opal glass petals held in gilded framework which housed the gas jets.

It is likely that much of the excitement of the splendid Pavilion was spoilt for most of the visitors, since the gas burned with a constant hissing noise and gave off a considerable degree of heat, an unpleasant addition to that already being radiated by the patent heating stoves which were a feature of the Pavilion and a technical advance greatly applauded by the Prince.

Heat was also generated by the many candles and oil lamps which were in use throughout the building during the evening, so that few of the guests could have felt entirely comfortable in the formality of their attire or by the close proximity of their fellow guests, especially on the occasion of a ball or a banquet.

No doubt a good deal of discomfort was not thought out of place for the privilege of dining beneath the central chandelier which had cost £5,613, weighed almost one ton, and measured thirty feet from top to bottom (Plate 60).

Technical improvements in lighting by both oil and gas were features of the Regency, features which were of interest to the Royal Household in its demands for high fashion and scientific invention,

60 *Gaselier, Royal Pavilion, Brighton.*

but the old King, lost in the grip of insanity and away from the affairs of State, barely noticed the Empire style reaching its zenith during his time, and in this unhappy plight, he died, leaving the Prince of Wales to be crowned George IV (1820–30).

Not all chandeliers were as elaborate as the one mentioned above; in fact, the less pretentious fitting was, in its own way, beautifully plain and with few embellishments, relying entirely on proportion and flow of line for its appeal. An extant design typical of the period is composed of a large bun-shaped body surmounted by a large capped urn, and terminated below by a handsome finial. Vase-shaped candle sockets, gadrooned on the under side and

skirted by a wide lip, stand importantly on the end of 'door-knocker' arms, which are a feature of the later Georgian period (Plate 61).

By this time a new addition had been made to the selection of crystal drops now available for dressing chandeliers. The architect J. B. Papworth, tiring of the icicle and almond drops so long in vogue, designed some new pendants to compliment the new taste. Among these was a long, three-cornered pendant of clear glass, suspended from a single crystal button. These were used mostly on table candlesticks and candelabra, suspended closely around the sconces and almost obscuring the central shaft by a heavy fringe of glass – the ancestor to the Victorian lustre.

From this oblong 'prism' drop, a London glasshouse developed the 'ruler' drop, a long pendant, flat on one side and convex on the other, and vase ornaments appeared with glass pendants hung from their rims; even metal chandeliers were lavishly

61 *Georgian 'door knocker' chandelier, 1820/30.*

dressed with crystal garniture. Chandeliers in wood were also heavily garlanded, overlaid with acanthus, and had their candle arms springing from the top of lions heads. The wide sconces were mounted on a gadrooned support and upheld fluted sockets with a milled edge.

Black banding was used extensively to emphasise gilt or silver decoration, and wall brackets were made with the ebony female figure rising from a tapering pedestal picked out in gold leaf. A pair of figures, male and female, draped or nude, would also be used as candlesticks and made to uphold candle sockets either singly or in multiple arrays, and a figure of Atlas, bowed beneath the weight of a monumental candelabrum.

Generally, the light from a single chandelier was not expected to provide for the whole room; supplementary lighting was obtained by placing candelabra on pedestals or wall brackets wherever the light was most needed, and as by now there was no shortage of candles, the high society was able to provide as adequately as necessary for any occasion. For example, at one great ball there would be as many as 1000 perfumed candles burning at once, while at the other end of the scale a retiring guest would help himself to a single candle from the candle box at the foot of the stairs and light his way to the bedchamber.

By about 1830 the neatly and efficiently designed Student Lamp came in from France. This was built around the strength of a central brass rod standing on a bell-shaped foot. To one side of the rod was fitted an oil font containing colza oil which was gravity fed through a tube down to the reservoir mounted on the opposite side

of the lamp and supplying the oil to the Argand wick. The wick was protected by a chimney which also provided extra air-flow, and this was covered by a dome-shaped green shade which reflected the light downwards to the table surface. The whole unit was adjustable up and down its supporting rod.

Another highly-prized fitting from the French Empire was the table candelabrum fitted with a circular iron shade with sloping sides. Hanging fittings with this shade were also popular, and it was not long before the simple iron shade was adopted for other lighting devices such as candlesticks and lamps.

With the increasing use of oil lamps, the old candle-cupboard, at one time used exclusively for the household candles, became the storage place for lamps, chimneys, shades, wicks, trimmers and bottles of oil, and in this connection was eventually renamed the 'lamp room', sometimes to be housed in an outbuilding for safety.

The whaling industry, flourishing in the South Pacific and along the Californian coast, provided brightly burning whale oil for float-lamps and gravity-feed systems before the 1840s, and there were lamps made specially for whale oil burners with one, two or three wicks. They were made of brass, pewter or glass, the marine version being suspended in a wall-mounted gimbal so that the lamp remained vertical against the motions of the vessel.

Where fashion hardly ever dictated the style of household furnishing, people still used the candlesticks of their ancestors, and the old crusie which burned either fish oil or animal fats. In even remoter parts, the stone and shell lamps were still in service with those to whom candles remained unattainable luxuries.

Between 1835–40, rushes for making rush lights were sold by children at one penny a bundle. Beeswax candles were a shilling and twopence a pound; spermaceti candles, one shilling and eleven pence a pound. Tallow candles were about sixpence a pound and stearine were one shilling a pound. Cheaper candles were made by mixing rosin or cobbler's wax with new or old beeswax.

This was the time when a gentleman would live comfortably on a modest income, own a town house, possibly a country retreat, run a carriage and employ servants.

By comparison, a twelve-light, hand-carved chandelier in wood with gilt decoration, could cost between eighty and a hundred guineas. A simple brass chandelier could be purchased for between twenty and two hundred guineas. Candlesticks in brass were up to five guineas, and wooden candlesticks from a few pence up to thirty shillings or so.

Comparatively few gentlemen could lavish their income on fancy chandeliers, and none but the very wealthy, had glass ones. The candlestick served the needs of most people, rich and poor alike.

Georgian lanterns were especially well proportioned and beautifully decorated, less extravagantly than their French counterparts. Clear glass with an etched or painted design was sometimes used in the windows, but as the object of the lantern was to provide much-needed light, the glass was usually clear and unadorned. Usually a metal or glass smoke bell would be suspended above the lantern to protect

62   *Regency candle lantern, c.1820.*

the ceiling from the rising smoke of candles or lamps. Lantern frames were made in gold, brass, silver, bronze, copper, mahogany, lime wood, walnut, oak and glass. Shapes ranged from the cylindrical forms of the previous era to the later hexagonals and octagonals; straight-sided and tapering, or finely shaped with curving convex windows and often surmounted by a crown or coronet.

The changing form of Georgian lanterns can be seen by comparing the open overlaid framework of the earlier models, with the irregular flow of the rococo

(Plate 62), and the return of formality with leafwork overlaying the under frame and with the occasional cherub standing among the candles.

But while candlelight and lamplight vied for superiority in the changing scheme of Georgian interiors the increasing use of gas provided further possibilities for new designs and experiments. Both glass and metal chandeliers were converted so that gas burners could be used in place of candles, and as the incandescent mantle had not yet been invented, the gas burned as a naked flame, its shape being determined by the shape of the aperture through which the gas issued.

In the face of technical difficulties and a good deal of public distrust, the day was not far ahead when the gas engineer would become a professional technician, and when oil lamps would be packed away in the cellar or the attic as relics of a by-gone era.

REGENCY TO VICTORIA

The storm clouds of unrest had long been gathering. Trade and industry had fallen into a state of depression. Farm labourers revolted in the south. Industrial workers rioted in the north. The harvest was the worst for ten years. Unemployment was high, and cholera from the Continent threatened the land, as an age of splendour seemed to collapse with the death of George IV in 1830.

In this mood, the Hanover line continued with the accession of the Duke of Clarence as William IV. Because the reign was short (1830–37), it has become common practice among historians to group it with the following reign, or sometimes to class it as 'pre-Victorian', or to embrace the years 1830–60 as 'early Victorian'.

It does, however, bear closer attention as the transitional period during which the changes of the late Georgians evolved into the unsteady innovations of the early Victorians.

The inventive furniture makers of Georgian fame were all dead, and only a few contemporaries such as A. W. N. Pugin, Philip Hardwick, C. J. Richardson, Alfred Stevens and Owen Jones, showed evidence of ingenuity. It is not surprising that furniture design suffered for want of originality, since none of those gentlemen was predominantly a furniture designer or practical cabinet maker.

Fortunately not many people had discarded their chandeliers in favour of the new experimental gas brackets, for gas pervaded the already musty atmosphere with an odour no less objectionable than that from oil lamps, and besides emitting an irritating hiss, the fluctuating pressure caused the flame to rise and fall and sometimes to go out altogether.

The opening of gas works to supply gas for lighting and cooking had done much to stimulate the interest of small sections of curious citizens in most parts of the country, but the use of gas was governed by cost; it was not readily available, even to those prepared to afford it; and as the operation of the gas-producing plants was almost on a part-time basis, improvements had to be made in the matter of training and maintaining staff to keep pace with the increasing demand.

The workers who installed, assembled, modified and maintained the public gas lighting services in over 200 miles of

London streets were the original gas engineers and fitters, and it is from this time that the term 'fitting' became attached to lighting appliances, and such items as wall brackets and pendant lights were called 'gas fittings'.

Lighting fittings such as chandeliers, candelabra and table lamps could be modified by the new tradesmen so that the gas could be fed into the wick chamber of the oil lamps and into the socket of chandeliers which had been adapted to take the gas jet; and the regulating tap would allow gas to escape through the jet where it could be ignited from a lighted taper. But those burners which were made of iron quickly corroded, and the brass ones were only a little better, so that frequent replacement was necessary in the interests of a good light and a safe fitting.

The use of oil continued to occupy the thoughts of designers and inventors, but the Argand type of burner remained the most efficient invention to date, so much so that the principle had been adopted in some gas lamps and was marred only by the inefficiency of the burners available at that time.

Designs for lampadiers continued to be elaborate and individual, and many now burned the mineral oil available in regular but small consignments from Roumania and Burma.

A fashionable model of about 1835 had a short cylindrical body supported from a shaft coloured in dark green and relieved by polished brass applied motifs. The scroll arms terminated in cast iron rings into which fitted the glass, or brass, oil fonts of the lamps. A chimney over the wick chamber and an opal or green outer shade completed the often magnificent creation.

Even so, the lampadier began to make way for the gasolier; the lamp bracket's new brother was the gas bracket; the oil lamp became the gas lamp, and so on. Most of the original candle-burning fittings, however, had solid arms which at once excluded their use for conversion to gas, and this resulted in newly designed fittings with hollow arms, regulating taps, jets and gas pipes all built-in as an integral part of the construction.

Some designs were simple while others were more progressive and perhaps a little alarming in their concept. These included a human head with a burner in the skull, or a winged griffin spitting flame from its tongue, or an innocent little cherub holding a naked flame in the palm of his hand.

In contrast to chandeliers, lampadiers and gasoliers, many households had modified their use of burning candles and lamps throughout the night, and had adopted the more convenient night-light. This small, inexpensive article was a long-burning, squat candle which sat in a shallow measure of water in a decorated porcelain or glass bowl, sometimes protected by a short glass funnel. These were popular between 1830 and 1835, and were destined for even greater acclaim in the next era.

VICTORIAN

Lighting fittings were being made of steel and cast-iron as well as the established materials of the bygone periods, when the burden of State fell dramatically to the King's eighteen-year-old niece, Victoria (reigned 1837–1901); and furniture designs had fallen into a succession of classic 'revivals'; revivals which at least enables us to identify 'Victorian Gothic', 'Victorian Tudor', 'Victorian French' and so on through the passing of time.

Experts have long sought reasons for the sharp decline in designing and productive skills of the early period, and at one time it was generally thought 'intellectual' to reject the entire period as tasteless and vulgar; but one cannot so easily dismiss the achievements of three-quarters of a century, and a closer study will reveal to most of us that all which is ugly is not Victorian and all which is Victorian is not ugly.

The nation-wide use of candles and its love of candle-light persisted throughout the era, even after the advent of paraffin for lamps and the slowly spreading demand for gas, but as many households had decided that gas lighting was something 'not quite nice', or at best 'inelegant', continued business was ensured for the chandler, the candlestick maker and the chandelier builder.

Moreover, there were certain spheres of activity in which only candles or oil lamps would suffice, and one of these was reserved exclusively for sea travel. Life aboard the sea-going vessel had always been hazardous and none too comfortable, and managing the lighting arrangements was perhaps the most inconvenient task on even the most uneventful voyage.

Aboard the *Britannic* of 1840 the list of instructions to passengers included the rule that they had to '. . . quash the candles in their staterooms at midnight.' Many a saloon deck was lighted by simple hanging candle lanterns, and an illustration of the *Great Western* shows just such a lantern, constructed of wrought iron with a hurri-cane shade over the candle. There are also references to the 'dismal light of spluttering candles, extinguished by the steward when ever the captain says so,' and to the '. . . sooty slush lamp that swings from the beams.'

In most liners the bulkhead candles and the saloon lamps were extinguished at 11 o'clock, and as soon as a storm seemed imminent the captain gave instructions for all lights to be extinguished immediately, which meant a hurried combined operation between the passengers and crew to put out all the interior lights before the storm enveloped the vessel.

Even Brunel's latest masterpiece of marine engineering, the *S.S. Great Britain*, which had been launched in 1843, was no more advanced in lighting techniques than were her predecessors.

The forerunner of modern steamship design, the *S.S. Great Britain* was three times the size of any ship before her. Her smooth hull was constructed entirely of iron, and her six sail masts were augmented by a single funnel amidships from which poured the smoke from her boilers when she was under steam. The single screw-propeller represented the first break from paddle-wheels; her wire rigging offered two thirds less resistance to the wind than the rope rigging of older ships, the engine room was the delight of engineering enthusiasts, and her five watertight bulkheads not only strengthened the ship but added considerably to her safety in the event of structural damage.

Her promenade deck and saloon, in which 300 persons could dine at one sitting, were simple but decorative, and a special 'ladies suite' enabled unescorted females to spend the entire voyage within the confines of this frilly sanctuary without the necessity of mixing with other passengers. The significance, here, is the gap between brilliant engineering and the obligation of the designer to adhere to conventional everyday lighting devices, for as we are able to see by contemporary illustrations, both the promenade and saloon decks were lighted throughout by simple two-arm hanging candle holders fitted between the sky-lights.

Also there is no reason to suppose that there was any deviation from the common practice of providing each stateroom with a wall-mounted brass or copper lantern case to house a small oil lamp or candle. There would also have been a simple, perhaps adjustable, candle bracket fitted near the bunk or washing-stand.

Officer's quarters, galleys, passageways etc., would have been equipped with gimble-mounted oil lamps fitted to the bulk-heads, each lamp having mounted above its glass chimney a metal smoke bell (Plate 63). The ward-room and Captain's cabin would probably have been fitted with hanging oil lamps suspended from a hook in the ceiling, while the crew would have used the simple blown-glass candle lantern swinging from a beam.

Nevertheless, it was inevitable that the emergent gas lighting should eventually be taken afloat, and during the 1850s gas installations were made in certain ships, amongst them the *S.S. Great Britain*. But such a sophisticated means of illuminations was confined to the public rooms, and was probably as unreliable as gas lighting ashore.

In returning to the more domestic aspect

of our story, and in consideration of the pending discovery of petroleum, it serves no useful purpose to further analyse the extensive use of candles, except that mention must be made of the night lights as made by Samuel Clarke of Childs Hill, London, from about 1860. His night light was a squat, slow-burning candle which lasted up to ten hours continuous burning. It was fitted into a decorative glass or metal base, something like a modern meat paste jar. Some were more elaborately decorated than others, and some were so beautifully shaped and cut with patterns that they were used as centre pieces for

63   *Marine lamp, c.1860.*

the dinner table, or as hanging chandeliers, an innovation which lasted well into Edwardian times. But mostly they were used in the nursery, bedchamber, sick room and in passages or on stairways.

The many variations on the glass shades included the acorn pattern, diamond cut, hob-nail cut, plain rose coloured glass, opaline and satin glass, and were patented under the name of 'Cricklight', 'Fairylite' and 'Pyramid.' Many glass shades of these night lights were made by Osler of Birmingham and Thomas Webb of Stourbridge, and many bases were made by Palmer & Co., London.

Interest in other lighting devices was sharply arrested when, in 1859, Colonel Drake sank wells in Pennsylvania and tapped tremendous supplies of rock-oil; oil of the kind noted by Marco Polo in the thirteenth century during his remarkable travels through lands now known as the Baku oil fields.

In the meantime, two Americans, Weston Howard and Samuel Kier, had invented a process of refining the crude oil, and by their process of distillation they were able to separate the complex mixture into various constituents, of which paraffin is one. This proved to have such ideal properties as an illuminant that it at once became known as 'lamp oil', and although more expensive than previously used oils, it did not deteriorate, it rose easily up a lamp wick by capillary action, emitted less smoke, did not smell, and was relatively clean, for which reasons it immediately became the standard lamp oil to which most existing lamps were easily adapted.

One advantage of paraffin was that a lamp could use a single broad wick, which allowed for a simple cog-and-spindle raising and lowering system. In fact a whole new range of lighting equipment was made possible since it was no longer necessary to raise oil to the wick by clockwork

64   *Paraffin lamp, c.1868.*

motors, or to gravity-feed it from a raised font, or to make do with a meagre light if neither of these systems were used. In 1865, the introduction by Hinks of the double-burner, with the two ribbon wicks side by side provided a method which produced an even greater light output.

Designs for new paraffin lamps tended to be over elaborate, and one may well see a Baroque style four-footed pedestal with a circular table-top of marble bearing an ormolu urn heavily decorated with rococo foliage, on top of which was mounted a glass oil font with a duplex burner; the wick chamber being covered with a chimney and a decorated outer shade of etched glass (Plate 64). Cheaper models were made with a simple brass or tin font mounted on a trumpet or domed foot, the flame protected by a chimney and an opal glass shade which people often referred to as 'moon'.

Common amongst outdoor lamps were the naphtha flares of the street traders and road repairers, and the hurricane lamps of the 1880s. There was also the curiously formed, cast-iron Wells kettle torch, some-times called a 'slush' lamp. This was shaped like a large coffee pot with a carrying handle and a lid, and a wide upturned spout. The spout held a thick rag wick that trailed down into the body, which was charged with any oily waste available, and could be topped-up with train oil as required to maintain the fierce flame that shot from the spout.

Most middle-class houses were equipped with one or more lamp cabinets for use along corridors and in hall ways. This was essentially a square or tall cabinet made of polished brass, tin or copper, with bevelled glass windows and a smoke ventilator at the top. A handle enabled the cabinet to be carried, and it could be inserted into the lantern case above the street door, or put safely on to a convenient wall bracket or shelf anywhere in the house. In earlier times it housed a candle or float lamp, but was now put to use for the small paraffin lamp.

The lamp room with all the component parts required for the oil lamps of the residence, was now being re-arranged to accommodate the extra impedimenta needed to maintain the gas fittings. Glass shades, chimneys, cleaning materials, and replace-ment burners costing a guinea each, were held in stock at all times.

It was not until 1858, when Sugg patented his invention of the steatite orifice, which would not corrode, that the difficulty in maintaining gas fittings was largely overcome, and the subsequent success of gas as a lighting medium, both internally and externally, brought the greatest revolution in lighting that had ever been possible.

Hundreds of designs for burners had been evolved, but since they had all suffered from the defects of corrosion only those with the new steatite orifice were used on new fittings, although not every burner in use was immediately exchanged for the improved model. There were brass burners dating from about 1812, iron burners from the 1820s, and burners of steatite from about 1858. Burners were designed to give different shapes to the flame, and there was the Union jet, the duplex burner, the rat's tail, the bat's wing and the fish tail (Plate 65); in all, seven types of burner being in general use.

In the place of oil-burning table lamps,

65 *Fishtail gas burners at Billingsgate fish market, London.*

there were designs for gas-burning table lamps, many of which were based on models of candlesticks and oil lamps (Plate 66). The well known Argand system of passing air through the centre of the burner to increase the intensity of the flame was also adopted for gas burners, and up to 1,200 candle-power, and from gasoliers, in the installations using this principle. From table lamps one might expect about 19 candle-power, and from gaseliers, in the region of 50 candle-power.

The Sugg Christiana burner of 1874 made possible a selection of newly designed table

66   *Gas table lamp, c.1874.*

lamps with more slender stems which were fitted at the top with ornate brackets to hold inner and outer shades. A flexible pipe fed gas into the stem and up to the burner.

Those involved in the development of gas lighting were aware of the need to exercise more control over the flame after it had left the orifice, and Gurney in 1826, Drummond in 1828 and Clamond in 1882, had all evolved models of the incandescent mantle, but it eventually fell to Dr. Carl von Welsbach of Vienna to produce the most practical model to date, using in its production a mixture of rare earths which he had introduced as early as 1885.

In 1893, the mantle was made more efficient by the addition of thorium oxide to the ceria, and by 1897 the newly formed 'Incandescent Gas Light Company' was selling burners and mantles in Westminster.

Compared with the open flame, the new mantle gave a brilliant white light from which 60 to 70 candle-power was being achieved. Most lamps from about 1893 were therefore fitted with the mantle which to this day is produced to the identical design.

A significant development in gas fittings was the rise-and-fall gasolier which dates from the 1850s. The construction enabled the entire unit to be raised closer to the ceiling when not in use, and lowered when light was required in the main part of the room.

These were often elaborate with traditional motifs and leafwork, consisting of a central tube sliding inside another which contained a water seal to prevent the gas escaping. The lower end of the outer tube was attached to the body of the fitting which carried the arms, taps and burners.

It will be remembered that rooms were generally high, and that the standard type of gas fitting shed more light in the upper half of the room that in the lower half where it was most needed, since all jets at that time had to burn in an upright position.

Ceiling and wall decoration of the period was of sombre colouring, there being little reflected light, and therefore the rise-and-fall gasolier overcame the disadvantages of other models which were fixtures. Technical difficulties resulted in the late development of a downward burning orifice, and it was not until between 1900 and 1903 that the inverted burner was developed, together with a new method of attaching the mantle and a different method of controlling the flame.

From the Paris Exhibition of 1867, there came to England a wide selection of beautiful gasoliers, brackets and table lamps, all exceptionally ornamental and made of brass, bronze, iron and silver plate. The metal work was deeply moulded, chiselled and finely chased to add brilliance and interest to their decoration. Body and arms were overlaid with acanthus leaf, oak leaf or ivy, and contained all manner of traditional motifs such as the anthemion, birds, human figures, shells, foliage, dragons and Egyptian and Gothic designs.

There had been nothing like the manufacturing quality and decorative exuberance in the history of mass-produced lighting fittings, and since fittings could be made as simple or as elaborate as the purchaser wished, there were prices to suit almost everyone. Everyone, that is to say, except for the very poor and very remote, who still used the paraffin lamp,

cheap candles or even fats to shed light in their humble dwellings. Naked gas jets burned in the tenements and most schools. Many houses, even better class ones, often had gas light in only the main living rooms, the rest being served by lamp or candle as thought to be appropriate.

The demand for decorative glass shades opened a new branch of manufacture in the glass industry, and there were countless variations of design to be had from the shops. Many were in clear glass, cut in the established patterns of glass workers. Others were hand painted by prominent artists as well as by many amateurs, and it became the 'genteel' pastime of talented young ladies to decorate gas globes for relatives and friends.

All manner of designs were to be found, including landscapes, floral patterns, wild life, children at play, ships, and scenes of general pictorial interest.

Out of doors, the main road of towns and cities, and some villages, were becoming brilliant with the newly developed street lighting, and the names of Sugg, Chandler, Schulke and Wenham are but a few among the many who applied for patents for outdoor lighting.

From humble beginnings as a simple naked flame contained within a glass and metal case, street lighting had become one of the sights of the town. Parties of interested persons would make their way out by night, to point out to each other the merits of the different designs, and to identify them by their official names. There was the 18-inch Victoria, the 38-inch Lambeth, the 44-inch Lambeth, the 16-inch Windsor, the 16-inch South London, the Westminster, the Lucas Intensive gas lamp, and the Rochester, all familiar sights by the end of the era. The light value of each lamp was in the region of 300–400 candle-power, a startling improvement on all other street lighting devices.

The elegant society persisted in its taste for crystal and crystal chandeliers, and there were glass candlesticks, sweetmeats and vases draped with long crystal pend-ants which the Victorians called *lustres* after the French term for chandelier.

The long prism-cut drops of the Empire days were now given some new shapes. Patterns were cut into the prism, and the lower end nipped into a slender waist above an octagonal arrow-head of crystal. Inevitably, this elegant creation was christened the 'Albert' drop, which ensured its popularity if only for patriotic reasons, but as the Albert drop was indeed a beautiful piece in its own right it soon inspired the fashionable middle class popu-lation to introduce changes into the drawing room.

Many older chandeliers that had survived from earlier times were stripped of their original dressing, and had their almond and icicle drops replaced by the long tinkling Alberts, and new chandelier designs were originated to satisfy the fresh demand.

It is, perhaps, unfair to have come so far through our story without mentioning two notable systems which, although unsuited to domestic use, and far from decorative, were nevertheless important steps into the production of bright-light sources: namely the lime-light and the arc-light. We have, however, been somewhat pre-occupied with the evolution of more decorative lighting fittings.

Throughout these early developments there were no lighting engineers, and few people were engaged specifically on the design of lighting appliances, and so invention and design fell largely to persons of forethought and vision whose pro-fessional interests were often widely separated from the technology of lighting.

This was the case with Captain Thomas Drummond (1797–1840), a civil engineer in Edinburgh, who at one time was employed in the trigonometrical survey of Great Britain and Ireland. In 1825 he discovered that an intensly brilliant white light could be produced by directing an oxy-hydrogen flame upon a piece of lime, thus heating it to incandescence.

This became known as the Drummond Light, and by 1839 had been introduced into the popular Vauxhall Gardens and other open spaces in London as flood-lighting. It took until about 1856 before someone fitted a focussing lens over the front of the lamp-housing in order to make a spot-light, this system being subsequently used at the Princesses Theatre, London. After this the 'lime-light' became a stand-ard piece of equipment in most theatres for lighting-up the performers, and was frequently used out of doors for entertain-ments such as fairs, circuses and pleasure gardens.

Next we come to Sir Humphrey Davy (1778–1829), the great English chemist and professor at the Royal Institution, London from 1802–1812. Famous for his invention of the miners' safety lamp in 1816, Sir Humphrey's passion for science turned his attentions to the production of electric light, and in 1808–09, he had demonstrated his battery-activated carbon arc. Although the batteries, banks of bichromate cells, were unable to sustain the electric arc for very long, the first steps had been taken in the production of light by electricity.

There was news from Paris as early as 1841–4 that arc-lights, operating from bichromate cells, were being demonstrated in the streets with a view to developing a permanent installation. But those, and further demonstrations in London, Sunderland and Liverpool between 1848 and 1849, were not practical enough to encourage the use of the electric arc, and the matter was virtually shelved until a better power supply source could be developed.

There was, however, a remarkable invention which was destined, at last, to provide a sustained electricity supply; this was the electric dynamo, the Gramme Machine of 1870 being one of the most notable for its overall efficiency. The advent of dynamos allowed the principle of the electric arc to be perfected for outdoor use, and was to make possible the development of domestic electric light before the end of the century.

In the meantime, sceptics failed to recognise the importance of the work being carried out by Joseph Swan in his endeavours to produce an efficient system of lighting by electricity. Swan was developing the electric lamp in which a filament was raised to incandescence within a glass bulb from which the air had been exhausted by means of a vacuum pump.

Swan demonstrated his invention of the carbon filament lamp to a meeting of the Newcastle-upon-Tyne Chemical Society in December 1878, following-up in the following year with lectures at Sunderland and Gateshead, and crowning his tour with a large-scale exhibition in Newcastle on October 20th 1880.

To ensure his understanding of the principles of installation and maintenance, Swan lit his own house by electricity, and followed this by carrying out his first commercial installation in the business premises in which he had worked as a lad of eighteen, the chemist shop of Mawson and Swan.

Swan's Electric Light Company Limited of Newcastle immediately came under the patronage of progressive thinkers, the first of these being the wealthy industrialist Sir William Armstrong, who engaged Swan to light his mansion at Cragside, Rothby, in 1880.

As yet there were no public generating stations, and any installation had to be self-powered from its own generator. In this case Swan decided to use a six-horse-power turbine activated by the strong flow of a small stream three-quarters of a mile away from the house, and driving a Siemens' dynamo to deliver the electric current into the building by means of copper conductors.

In the dining room, a centre fitting housed six lamps inside a single opal glass shade, and a bracket lamp on each side of the room extended the illumination as far as the walls (Plate 67).

On the staircase, carved wooden beasts which were part of the existing woodwork were adapted to hold posts which carried the new electric lamps, and the picture gallery was served by no less than thirty-two lamps, twelve being available for operation at all times, and a further twenty coming into service when the current had been shunted from the dining room when it was no longer required. Developments

67   *Swan's installation of 1880 at Cragside.*

succeeded experiment on both sides of the Atlantic, and in 1883 Swan merged with Thomas Edison in London to form the Edison-Swan United Electric Light Company, through which they planned to provide electricity on a national scale.

London was not far behind when it came to adopting new ventures, and in 1886–7 the Kensington Court Generating Station opened and provided electricity for only three houses in the district. But improvements were on the way, and the success of electric lighting was to become Edwardian rather than Victorian.

EDWARDIAN

The Art Furniture movement of the 1870s and the 1880s had been dedicated towards better development in furnishings, and by the turn of the century new furnishing shapes were evident in the style of the *art nouveau,* and in particular in the swing towards an Anglo-Japanese style in trend-setting circles.

Even so, the background remained predominantly Victorian, and the reign of Edward VII (1901–10) is still regarded as the days of red plush and gaslight, although no household was complete without its selection of paraffin lamps and candlesticks.

The average middle-class house had gas brackets on each landing; centre fittings and brackets in principal rooms; a gas jet in the lamp-case over the street door, and a pair of street lanterns on the gate posts. Less important rooms, for which no gas supply was available, had either paraffin lamps or candlesticks made of brass or Sheffield plate.

As dusk approached, a servant would commence to light up the residence. The gate lanterns had a pivotted gas cock with chains attached for ease of handling, a pull down on one side released the gas into the jet, a pull down on the opposite side shut it off.

Before the introduction of the pilot-light, which ignited the gas as soon as it was turned on, the servant had to climb a set of portable steps to ignite the gas with a match, but many households possessed a lamp-lighter's torch-stick for this purpose.

A principal bedroom had a centre gas fitting depending from a decorated plaster ceiling rose, the pipe terminating in a simple opal glass shade through the open bottom of which the taper was offered to the gas jet. The pivotted gas-cock was operated by the manipulation of chains. The servants, according to status, had brass or tin candlesticks, the most senior amongst them being allowed the privilege of a paraffin lamp.

In those houses where the family still preferred the more traditional atmosphere, the dining room would have been served by candelabra, supplemented, perhaps, by lamps set close to the walls on lamp tables. The pride of many an Edwardian residence was a glass candelabrum made especially for holding the tiny night-light candles made by Samuel Clarke & Co., and this was used as a centre piece for the dining table on most occasions.

As electricity began to replace gas in some districts, so the electric light bulb shed its unflickering rays from within the lamp case over the street door, staring steadily at its big electric brothers now lining the streets.

Shades for electric light pendants were large and domed, with long fringes of

Lighting manufacturers made fittings for either gas, candles or electric lamps according to choice, so that a fine reproduction silver Knole or Haddon Hall fitting could be had as a chandelier, or as a gasolier, or as an electrolier – the latest in lighting terminology.

The gasolier, with its tubular arms, became an ideal subject for conversion to electricity, with wiring inside the arms, lampholders in the place of gas jets, lamps in the place of mantles and pretty little glass shades to add decorative effect, most of which were, in fact, gas-light shades. Lamp-stands could be converted to electric standard lamps, and even the Victorian pole-screen was turned into a chair-side lamp.

But long before the urge for converting existing fittings had subsided, manufacturers were making electroliers for every situation and occasion. A domestic table lamp of the period was a simple baluster stem mounted on a short column rising from a circular base raised on feet. The shade which fitted over the lampholder was described as being of oriental design, and consisted of a number of vertical panels surmounted by a shallow dome.

An electrolier in a public building was basically a large cut-glass dish held in a decorative ormolu band which was suspended from six lengths of rod from a ceiling plate. Around the circumference of of the ormolu band six winged cherubs' heads held pendant glass bowls which contained the electric light bulbs (Plate 68).

Many exceptionally well designed electroliers were to be seen in department stores, hotels and other public buildings,

68   Edwardian electrolier.

beads or silk. New, smaller-scale crystal balloon fittings were also made to house electric lamps. There were waterfall fittings with icicle drops, Alberts or ruler drops; and baguettes of every convenient size were made by the established lighting manufacturers with showrooms and workshops in London and Birmingham.

Lighting showrooms were extremely decorative and museum-like, having all their fittings, brackets and standard lamps on show in well organised displays through which the prospective purchaser would be conducted by sales staff after the manner of museum guides.

electroliers were to be seen in department stores, hotels and other public buildings, and especially new passenger liners, bound for the Atlantic routes, which were fitted with magnificent lighting arrangements that rivalled the finest ashore.

The *Mauretania* was an undisputed queen of the seas, but rising rapidly in the stocks at the Belfast shipyard of Harland and Wolff was the giant framework of the *R.M.S. Olympic,* and reside her, the *R.M.S. Titanic,* sister ships that were to make maritime history in their day.

The *Olympic* was due for launching in the October of 1910, and when completed would steam across the Atlantic shimmering in the halo of her own electric light. Deep down in the great hull there were four engines and dynamos that could maintain a one-hundred-percent switch-on throughout the ship, serving her 10,000 lamps with a 100-volt supply day and night.

The First Class Dining Saloon had gilt and crystal electroliers on the ceiling, and matching three light brackets on the walls; and each table was provided with a shaded table lamp. In the à la carte Restaurant, the crystal electroliers were complemented by ormolu multi-light wall brackets, standing off the French walnut panels in the form flaming torches, and costing in the region of £200 each. Table lamps with pink silk shades lit each table with a subdued glow. On the lower newel post of the Grand Staircase, aft and forward on A Deck, and repeated in the Reception Room on D Deck, was a bronze boy, holding aloft a flaming torch (Plate 69).

Lighting in the staterooms was by means of cut glass ceiling bowls, wall brackets and

69   Bronze boy, *R.M.S.* Olympic, *1910.*

table lamps, and each room was reproduced in a different style. The table lamps, while being of similar design, were not an exact replica of each other, but showed variations on the basic theme. Most of the lamps were lyre-shaped, gimble-mounted on a domed base and supporting a central shaft which held the lamp and shade. A special feature of these lamps was the two-filament bulb which could be dimmed to provide a low-powered light as a night light.

Most of the decorative lighting fittings were made by the London lighting specialists Messrs A. Burt & Co., who in later years combined with the old firm of Perry & Co., who had made the lighting for the Royal Pavilion at Brighton.

Although the design and skilful building of the *Olympic* belonged to the Edwardian era, her launching date was still five months ahead when the King died in the May of 1910, leaving to his heirs and successors the romantic era of gas-light and red plush, Hansom cabs and the increasing popularity of electricity.

In leaving our story of lighting in England at this point one is apt to contemplate the significance of the fact that this was the last reign in which the monarch's name is directly identified with the period.

CHAPTER FIVE

America

The New World, as it was once named, has its own fascinating ancient history, established by the rich and talented civilisations of the Aztecs, the Mayas and the Incas, but the mediaeval period known in Europe and the far Continent is absent, a factor that limits the student of antiques to the Seventeenth and Eighteenth Centuries.

During the years it took to explore the country and to establish a community of planters, farmers and builders, Europe had enjoyed her Gothic, her Renaissance and her Baroque, and was entering her more expansive era of culture and trade; and since none of the notable craftsmen from Europe cared to join the emigration to the unknown Americas, matters of quality and fashion were governed by the standard and style of imported goods.

COLONIAL

In Colonial days, Virginia, Jamaica, New England and New York became predominently English. New Jersey and Pennsylvania, essentially Dutch. California and Florida were Spanish, and Louisiana was French.

Both furniture and lighting fittings among the settlers during the Seventeenth and Eighteenth Centuries were of the most rudimentary kind, the common possessions being the open oil pan and the rushlight holder.

The rushlight holder was a simple iron shaft embedded in a wooden base, and a roughly fashioned socket on one of the rush pincers could be used for a candle when such a luxury became available (Plate 70).

In the South it was possible to extract the heartwood of dead pine trees and to burn it in the fireplace for heat or in fire baskets for light. For portable purposes splinters of pitch pine could be bundled together and carried as a torch, giving off a bright spluttering flame and fragrant black smoke. They called this 'light wood', which is a fair indication of its widespread use for that purpose.

Elsewhere there was a continuous need for 'candlewood', which, we assume, was

70   Rush holder.

71   Double-pan crusie.

burned in fire pans or held in the hand after the manner of the European splint, but the fact that rushlight holders are more in evidence than the smaller splint holders, would indicate that candlewood was more widely used as a kindling wood than for lighting purposes.

The open oil pan was related to the Spanish *candil*, the French *candile* and the Scottish crusie, and at some time during its early use in America was given the name of 'Betty Lamp'. This was basically an open pan, pinched to a spout for the wick at one end and attached to a vertical hanging rod at the other (Plate 71). It is claimed that this type of iron lamp was taken across in the Mayflower in 1620, but the origin of the name given to it after its arrival remains obscure.

There was also the 'Ipswich Betty' and

the 'Newburyport Betty', which were essentially native products based on the originals. A more sophisticated crusie was made with a second pan suspended immediately below the first so as to catch the overflow of oil dripping from the spout, and this was called the 'Phoebe' lamp.

Later lamps were made of tin, copper and brass with many variations of design, but iron models remained the most durable and functional of the Betty lamps.

The more fortunate families possessed the table-standing Lucerna from the Netherlands. This being an oil-burning lamp on the principle of the Roman spout lamp, and having several wick-spouts protruding from its font. The font was adjustable up and down a central brass rod which attached the assembly to a heavy domed foot. A ring attached to the top of the rod enabled the lamp to be carried about or hung from a hook in the ceiling.

In 1697, the first street lighting ordinance was passed in New York, and ordained by decree that 'every seven householders should unit to pay the expense of burning a candle in a lantern suspended on a pole from the window of every seventh house on nights when there was no moon'.

Even with this facility the streets were by no means bright enough for comfort, and most of those obliged to journey by night took with them their personal lanthorn, rush torch, or bulls-eye lantern to make the night a little brighter. The lanthorn was a metal or leathern lantern with scraped horn for the windows; and the bulls-eye lamp with a glass window was the prized possession of only a few. But there were plenty of candlesticks made of brass, tin and enamelled metals for use inside the house, and these were carefully tended to keep them in good order and ready for the approaching night.

Factors common to most candlesticks of the mid-Seventeenth Century were the large grease pan set almost half-way up the stem, and a large trumpet base. Ringed pewter and latten candlesticks with a wide lip around the candle socket were common property, and at one time were given a Mayflower pedigree, although no one is certain of its authenticity (Plate 72).

Originally, glass played a relatively small

72 *Mayflower candlestick, Seventeenth Century.*

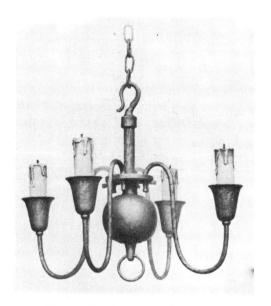

73 *Wood and metal chandelier, c.1700.*

part in the homes of the colonisers, but by 1750 there were glass works in Massachusetts, New Jersey and Pennsylvania, all making lantern glass, window glass, oil lamps and a variety of hurricane shades to fit over candlesticks.

The lighting arrangements out of doors remained somewhat crude, being confined to candle or oil lanterns. In New York City in 1762, the first public street lighting was erected and maintained at the expense of the city. This lighting was provided by lamps hanging from wooden posts set at intervals along the streets.

The lamps burned turpentine as the illuminant and were tended by a regular staff of lamp lighters who went about every morning carrying a can of oil, scissors and a supply of wicks. Mounted on the small ladders which they carried with them they blew out and trimmed the wicks, then topped-up the font with oil ready for the next night's service. At dusk, they commenced their rounds again and lit the lamps by means of torches. This went on until about 1823, when the introduction of gas lighting began to provide a gradual replacement for street oil lamps – which, however, were still lit by hand.

Most large residences had servants, and most public buildings had attendants, whose job it was to look after the lighting arrangements, in much the same way as we employ electricians today, and it was a frequent occurrence for evening dinner or a public function to be interrupted while the 'light men' attended to the snuffing of candles in the chandeliers, or dashed to the aid of someone who had been burned by tallow dripping from above.

By 1760 there were glass chandeliers from England, imported in their component parts in well-padded crates and assembled on site by carefully supervised servants. In contrast with the fine crystal pendants and swags of buttons on these expensive chandeliers, the lesser residence made do with a crudely made hanging fitting of doubtful origin, but commonly ascribed to either Holland or England. In this, a wooden shaft was fitted through the centre of a metal sphere or spherical wooden block to form the body of the fitting. Scrolled arms radiated from a metal block which was fitted to the shaft, and deep, flared sockets mounted at the end of each arm held the candles and served also to catch the dripping wax (Plate 73).

Metal chandeliers in Georgian styles were owned by the ruling classes, and many of those were copied in wood by local workmen to become products typical of their age and country. For standing in halls and corridors there were oil lamps with glass shades, or candle brackets for the wall, and hanging lanterns made of brass or tin. Wrought iron candle-stands on tripod feet had an adjustable bracket to which the candle sockets were attached. Both England and France exported dining table lamps made of brass, glass or bronze, and many of these were hung with crystal pendants.

Whale oil was readily available from the Pacific and along the Californian coast, and glass lamps for whale oil were made in England and New York during the 1770s.

Certain types of metal 'matched' certain rooms and specific applications. In outside buildings such as barns, food stores and wash-houses, there was the lanthorn or the bulls-eye lantern, and when these were not available there would be a simple tin candlestick surrounded by a cylindrical metal screen to protect the candle. The kitchen had the iron Betty lamp suspended from a beam or hanging from an iron floor stand, and tin candlesticks with home-made candles completed the lighting equipment for that particular area of household activities.

The main bedroom, the library and the study were equipped with brass candelabra or iron candlesticks, while the lesser bedrooms had a ringed pewter candlestick or a whale oil lamp. The dining room and parlour usually displayed silver candelabra of the William and Mary – Queen Anne – George I periods, which touched the Colonial homes with rich dignity.

So much perished in the Revolution that little original furniture remains outside of museums and some old family homesteads. Pewter was taken for bullets; brass for cannon, iron for wheels, and silver or gold for finances. Houses were wrecked or burned to the ground, furniture was looted or burned in revenge as the parties fought for superiority. It is, therefore, fortunate for our studies that at least one small corner of the Country remains preserved as evidence of our ancestry.

As long ago as 1699 Williamsburgh, Virginia, became one of the first planned towns in America, and under the notable plan drawn up by the Governor Francis Nicholas it became an elegant showpiece of proportion and pattern, with trees, open greens, and neat gardens surrounding the houses.

The people of Eighteenth Century Williamsburgh furnished their houses in the English style, using English exports and American made copies. Now the original buildings have been restored and re-furnished in the period styles from the Stuarts to the end of the Eighteenth Century, a programme of restoration that has been under the supervision of Williamsburgh Restoration Incorporated since 1937, and which today enables the curious traveller to capture some of the atmosphere of the Colonial town.

Best quality materials and first-rate workmanship have gone into reproducing furnishings and fittings down to the last detail, and from a varied selection of lighting devices we can gain an accurate picture of lighting fittings as they were once used.

The fittings in Williamsburgh have been identified, not by their style or country of origin, but by the location in which they were used in the town's buildings. A brass chandelier identified as 'The Governors' Office Chandelier' has a large centre basin,

74 *Governor's Office chandelier.*

gadrooned around the base and bearing scrolled candle arms around its rim. Suspension is by four scroll-and-link chains attached to a decorative ceiling cup (Plate 74).

The 'Apothecary Shop Chandelier' is an example of Dutch style, with six serpent-head scroll arms radiating from the shaft. The candle sockets are typically tall and cylindrical, rising from shallow pans. The 'Raleigh Tavern Chandelier' is in similar style, but its S-scroll arms have small leaf points overshooting the curves, and there are knops in the centre of the arms. A three-tier wall bracket of later design shows short stubby candle sockets, deeper pans and longer off-shoots of rustic work.

The 'Printing Office Chandelier', by contrast, is in antique tin, painted either black or green to choice. The body is like two pointed cones set together with one point down and the other point up, the whole being suspended from metal loops. Simple flat pieces of tin, curving upwards and out to hold shallow pans, are the arms (Plate 75).

The 'Palace Kitchen Sconce' is a tin wall light for one candle set in a short cup in front of a decorated reflector. The 'Wythe House Lantern' is a hanging, inverted glass dome suspended from ornamental brackets on chain, and bearing three candles within. A smoke bell at the termination of the chains prevents soot rising to the ceiling (Plate 76). There is also the 'Watchman's Lantern', in antique tin, straight sided and pierced at the top with designs in the style of old Moorish lanterns.

There are the 'Governor's Palace Hall Lantern', the 'Guard House Lantern' (Plate 77), the 'West Carriage Gate Lantern', the 'Small East Carriage Gate Lantern', the 'Palace Saucer-back Sconce', and a simple double-arm sconce, with two scroll arms rising from a circular backplate to candle

75 *Printing Office chandelier.*

76 Wythe House Lantern.

the winning of independence and, later, the establishment of the Federal Government.

FEDERAL

Following the War of Independance, which began in 1775 and ended with the defeat of the British at Yorktown in 1783, the Colonial era drew gradually to a close, so that the early years of Federal decoration differed little from the latter years of Colonial.

There was certainly nothing new in the matter of lighting devices, since the selection of illuminants was distinctly limited and the vessels in which to burn them were limited in design to remaining suitably shaped for their particular application.

Rushlights, Betty lamps and candle lanterns continued to serve the poor, and chandeliers, candlesticks and oil-burning lamps served the rich. Whale oil lamps were

77 Guard House lantern.

sockets over which hurricane shades are fitted to protect the candles from the draught.

All of these interesting fittings are supported by an appropriate selection of candlesticks which trace the varying designs through the periods represented in Williamsburgh (Plate 78).

But nothing subsequent to the Colonial period quite changed the scene as much as

78   Colonial candlesticks.

a special acquisition, especially those made of glass, and as they were free-blown, neither pressed nor moulded, each lamp differed from its fellows.

All early whale oil lamps were short and squat so as to reduce the danger of their being knocked over, as well as to keep the wick close to the oil. Most of them were float lamps in which the wick was held in a short vertical tube supported in a cork disc which floated on the surface of the oil. As the thick oil did not rise easily to the wick by capillary action, the float needed occasional agitation to induce the oil to soak into the wick.

These are at least as old as the early 1780s, and many of them were peg lamps intended for standing in a suitable socket, such as might be provided by a candlestick socket or the neck of a bottle.

The first real improvement came from England in the 'Patent Lamp', an oil font with an oil-tight screw-on cover which also held the wick tube. This was patented in 1787 by John Miles of Birmingham, England, and was, in fact, an 'agitable' lamp which could safely be shaken to render the oil more fluid for absorption. It was also the first safety lamp in as much as that it could survive casual movement and would not burst into flames when knocked over.

Glass and tin peg-lamps were made with the wick tube held in place by a screw fixing, while others were made of cast brass or pewter, either in the shape of an urn or a short cylinder into the mouth of which was fitted the cover plate. Some were mounted on a short stem rising from a dished base with a carrying handle. The marine version was mounted in a gimbal so as to automatically adjust to the vertical position against the motions of the ship.

The whale oil lamps in use in America from about 1795 were generally known as 'Patent Lamps' or 'Agitable Lamps'.

Glass whale oil lamps were distinctive and decorative, being made of heavy moulded glass in a variety of shapes, but more usually the font was either cylindrical or hexagonal, moulded on to a circular or hexagonal foot with a knop in the stem. The fonts were variously decorated with moulded motifs such as the medallion-and-star, birds, animals or foliage. The mouth of the font was provided with the tight-fitting metal cap which held the wick tubes and wicks to complete the lamp.

They date from about, 1825, when the glass factory at Sandwich commenced work, through to about 1845, when camphene burning-fluid came into use, and because of its explosive nature required a safer lamp and re-designed burners.

Of all American glass, Wistar, Stiegal, Quincy and Sandwich are sought by collectors, as is Binnington ware in pottery, and candlesticks by Dummer of Boston.

In particular one must admire the ornamental hurricane shades used to protect candles from the draught. Some were large enough to cover both candle and candlestick, while others were made to sit in the sconce of a bracket or chandelier. They were made in a variety of shapes and were often tinted with colour, particularly on the upper edges which were finished in a frilly out-turning lip.

Decoration was achieved either by hand painting, cutting or etching, and a favourite method of colouring was to tint the frilly edges with rose pink, sky blue or emerald green. Those pretty yet functional accessories were the ancestors of the outer shades for oil lamps and the mantle shades for gas fittings.

Whereas the Argand lamp had not gained immediate favour at the time of its introduction in England in 1784, it at once appealed to the more progressive mood of contemporary Americans. Benjamin Franklin had already anticipated the invention a year or two earlier when he attempted to use a hollow rush as a wick, but failed to pursue the idea with more efficient wicks. Both Franklin and Thomas Jefferson were in France in 1784, and noted the use of a cylinder lamp using a cylindrical wick.

When Argand went to England with his invention he not only patented his design, but contracted with Boulton & Co., to manufacture its successors for the English market. The oldest Argand lamp we know was made by Boulton's in 1784, a handsome, silver-plated double lamp, which was purchased by Thomas Jefferson and taken by him to America as the latest thing in oil lamps.

Another noteworthy Argand lamp is the double-burner model used by Washington in his residence at Mount Vernon. This is silver-plated and mounted on a glass base, the font being directly above the base and the lamps being set at both ends of a horizontal bracket which is braced for support by simple scrolls.

There were also Argand lamps for standing on the mantelpiece and for mounting on the wall by means of brackets. Mantle lamps were being made in Boston and New York and were popular between 1820 and 1850, it being fashionable to use them in sets of three, a double-burner model in the centre flanked by a single burner at either end of the mantel.

The main objection to the design of Argand lamps was that the font cast heavy shadows, so that numerous attempts were made to eliminate this disadvantage. The Carcel lamp of 1798 used an Argand wick chamber fitted into the mouth of a glass oil font. The base of the font was fitted with a two-cylinder clockwork-driven pump which delivered oil up to the burner. Carcel patented an improvement of his lamp in France in 1800, but it was soon being copied in England and not long afterwards found its way to America under both English and French patents.

In 1808, Bordier-Marcet patented a lampadier which was basically a ring-shaped font fitted with several Argand burners, which he called 'Une Apparel Astral', so named because the light came from above, like brilliant stars mounted around a wheel. A table lamp patented in 1810 had a ring-shaped font feeding a central burner, and was fitted with the recently invented Phillips 'spiral wick raiser' and a glass shade.

In 1820, Phillips invented a ring-shaped font of wedge-shaped cross section which succeeded still further in diminishing the shadow. These lamps were mounted on a columnar base with an onion-shaped shade and were called 'sinumbra lamps'. Franchot's Moderator lamp of 1836, used a coiled spring to exert a downward pressure on a piston head which in turn forced the oil in the font upwards to the wick chamber.

A certain amount of excitement was caused by the introduction from England of the Paragon and Vesta lamps which burned turpentine, and it was not long before it was discovered that a mixture of turpentine and alcohol produced an even brighter flame. These devices were generally known as camphene lamps, being popular between 1830 and 1850, but because they proved dangerous when carelessly handled they had to be treated with more caution than other oil lamps.

In 1830, Isaiah Jenning took out a patent which specified the preparation of camphene as a lamp oil, and in 1835 Henry Porter registered a patent which christened the oil as 'Porter's Patent Portable Burning Fluid', a name widely used to identify the product until the advent of paraffin, so that one could ask at the oil shop for 'fifty cents-worth of burning-fluid', and would leave with a bottle of liquid so potentially dangerous that most insurance companies refused cover to anyone known to be using it.

Lamps for use with burning-fluid were fitted with a cover bearing two tapering wick tubes which were set at a slight angle from the vertical, so forming a V on top of the cap. Burning-fluid (or camphene) lamps were also provided with two metal caps attached to chains on the main body of the lamp, and these were used to extinguish the flames and to cap the tubes to prevent evaporation of the contents when not in use.

Whale oil lamps could easily be fitted with suitable burners and many were converted for use with burning-fluid. Often it is difficult to identify a whale oil lamp from a burning-fluid lamp, but basically the whale oil wick tubes are of larger diameter and have a slot through which to adjust the wick. Burning-fluid wick tubes are slimmer and taper towards the top to pinch the wick as it leaves the aperture.

Burning-fluid lamps also needed more stability than did whale oil lamps, and were generally fitted to a large dish base, with a finger loop for carrying (Plate 79). Burmese oil was imported via London, England, to New York, and thousands of gallons of this expensive oil came in every year. By the early 1840s the price of most lamp oils had soared to about $2·50 per gallon when purchased from the oil shops, but were a little cheaper direct from the docks where it was landed from abroad.

Whale oil was cheaper, and sea elephant oil could be bought for about 75c. per gallon, but not everyone could easily afford even the lowest prices then being asked for lamp oils.

In an effort to find a safe inexpensive oil, inventors turned their attentions to the soft lard commonly used in grease lamps, and in doing so found it necessary to devise new lamps in which the oil was kept warm and in a fluid state so that it could be soaked up by the wick.

Flat wicks held between metal holders which extended downwards into the oil was the principle of the simple lard oil lamp; the object being that the burning wick heated the conductors which in turn transmitted heat into the oil to keep it fluid.

It was, therefore, necessary to keep the oil font as close as possible to the source of heat and to keep the oil as close as possible to the wick. In 1854 a lamp

79   *Whale oil and camphene lamps, 1840s.*

patented in the United States by Smith and Stonesifer employed a screw-driven piston which, given a regular adjustment, would force the less viscous lard into a warming chamber where it would liquify and gently feed the wick.

Whale oil burners already had wick tubes that extended downwards into the oil, and it is likely that these too were used with lard oil, which in 1841 was obtainable for about 50c. per gallon, although it rose to 75c. during the next few years.

The most expensive, but probably the most efficient lard oil lamps were made with Argand burners, which continued to provide the brightest and most efficient light of all.

Both lighting and furnishing design saw few changes until the French Empire interpretation from England provided a new status symbol for the ruling classes in their endeavour to discard the old and put on the new. To this end they were inclined to make a clear break rather than mix Colonial and Federal styles, and so much was destroyed during this and other transitional periods that America had little chance of becoming rich in her own antiques.

Between 1790 and 1811, the eagle, with wings spread, appeared on chandeliers and wall lights, together with foliage and tassels, but most typical of the Federal period was the Antoinette mirror, a fascinating convex mirror in a circular frame made of carved and gilded wood, with a row of gold or ebony spheres encircling the inside of the frame next to the mirror's edge.

Surmounting this would be a gilt or ebony eagle standing poised for flight on

80 *Adam style chandelier, 1780s.*

elaborately carved acanthus leaves. Often the mirror frame was fitted with delicately shaped arms, which bore glass pans and candle sockets.

Glass chandeliers and candelabra in Adam and Empire styles took their places in richly decorated homes. Tall lead crystal chandeliers with long arms, and draped with swags of crystal buttons, hung in dining rooms and drawing rooms (Plate 80), and many were fitted with decorated hurricane shades to protect the candles from the draught, which at times, cut through those great Southern houses with considerable force. Nothing in Federal decoration is more appropriate than the use of these attractive candle shades, either plainly made or ornamented with floral designs or spread eagles.

Glass candlesticks were in profusion, being moulded and cut in all the popular shapes of the era, but the most expensive and perhaps the most skilfully made glassware was imported from Bohemia or from Waterford in Ireland.

Candlesticks with crystal pendants hanging around their glass sconces were made in Wedgwood's popular jasperware, and were generally called *lustres*. Wooden wall brackets, carved, ebonised and gilded in Sheraton style were featured in most rooms of the Federal period, and similar models were cast and chased on bronze or ormolu. Many of these designs incorporated an eagle standing on a plinth raised above candle holders which sprang like growing vines from a central foliage motif (Plate 81).

In general we may study English Empire and American Federal styles as one conception of fashion, furnishing and personal manners, in much the same way as we observe the Victorian influence from England as settlers came across with their crinoline dresses, balloon-back chairs and silver teapots.

When, in 1859, Colonel Drake sank the first oil well in Pennsylvania and tapped-off seamingly unlimited supplies of crude oil, a new era of lighting could be visualised by those who still pursued perfection for the oil lamp.

Weston Howard and Samuel Kier were next to contribute to the application of crude oil to domestic needs when, in 1860, they introduced a process for refining the

81   English Empire bracket, c.1800.

oil and separating it into several component parts, one of which was lamp oil, or paraffin, which is more commonly known in the States as kerosene.

It was not long before Samuel Kier's vast refinery at Titusville was producing kerosene in large quantities, so that lighting by kerosene lamp almost rivalled the novelty of lighting by gas, even in sophisticated New York. Here was a liquid fuel

82 Hitchcock lamp, 1880.

many of the more pleasing designs remained in service for many years. Furthermore, the discovery of kerosene gave a new lease of life to the flat wick, which could absorb the thin oil at a steady rate of burning while at the same time providing a good, bright flame.

The Student Lamp, made in France for colza oil in 1830, needed little modification to control the flow of kerosene into the wick reservoir, and that continued in use well into the 1870s.

It was not long, however, before the necessity to convert existing lamps was superseded by lamps made specially to handle the burning of the new lamp oil. Thousands of patents were applied for by inventors and would-be inventors, and probably just as many model lamps were made for approval, but it was the Hitchcock lamp of 1880 that proved to be the most efficient, although it was not the first of its kind to be marketed.

The idea had been patented in England by Halpin in 1840, and in the States in 1860, but it was probably due to the lack of a properly developed fuel that these earlier blower-assisted lamps remained undistinguished.

Within the base of the Hitchcock lamp, a clockwork-operated fan created a mild current of air that aerated the flame and eliminated the necessity of using a chimney to increase the draught, as was the case with most other oil burning lamps, although this theory was certainly modified in later models. Eventually, all other patents were absorbed by the firm of Hitchcock & Co., of Watertown, New York, so that Robert Hitchcock enjoyed the success of his lamp for many years (Plate 82).

that could be safely contained in the font, burned with a steady rate of combustion, and was thin enough to be absorbed by the wick without either internal pressure or the need for gravity feed systems.

This outdated the clockwork mechanism of the Carcel lamps, the spring pressure of the Moderator lamps and the gravity-feed oil fonts of even earlier models, but as most lamps were readily adapted to kerosene,

While the artificially produced draught was effective enough in assisting the wick to burn brightly, the flame could still be affected by external air currents, and for this reason it seems likely that more Hitchcock lamps were used with chimneys than is generally supposed, because many of them were fitted with a gallery around the wick housing to support a chimney or a decorated shade.

For more rugged conditions and for sheer durability, the familiar hurricane lamp of the 1880s proved to be a safe, reliable, kerosene-burning medium for both indoors and out, while in saloons, private residences and some public buildings there was a generous selection of lamps imported from European countries.

A hanging lamp of French origin had a brass font mounted with a white chimney and a metal, coolie-hat-shaped reflector held above the body on decorated scroll arms. A lamp of German origin had a large brass font bearing the wick chamber and chimney, and a large metal reflector shade supported within a hoop rose from the sides of the font and connected with the suspension chain above (Plate 83).

The variations were legion. Every type of lighting device was in use *somewhere* in the country, and fittings were poorly made or beautifully made according to price or individual needs, or, as often as not, according to their availability in different areas or districts. Hotels, saloons and other public buildings not yet converted to gas lighting, and discarding the more common single lamps or chandeliers, were quick to take up the more decorative lamps which came in from England, France or Italy.

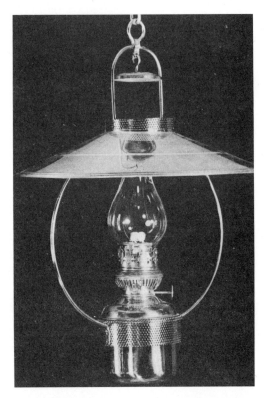

83 *Hanging lamp, German, Nineteenth Century.*

They came in *suites*, which included hanging lampadiers, table lamps and bracket lamps, and they had hand-painted porcelain or glass fonts capped by pretty glass shades, etched or cut with delicate patterns, and tinted around their frilly edges (Plate 84).

As we can appreciate from the widely ranging dates of our story, the development of lamps, lamp oils and burner systems, had occupied the thoughts of inventors for many centuries before the discovery of kerosene made it possible to produce an acceptable standard of lighting by oil lamps.

Alternative methods of providing light

84   Suite of lamps, Italian.

have always been under active consideration, and the Nineteenth Century was no
exception, for it brought us lighting by
gas within its first twenty years, and
lighting by gas and electricity during the
last twenty years was no less an innovation
than the Argand lamp or the kerosene
lamp, in fact, it proved a formidable
opponent.

The industry of manufacturing gas for
lighting had its practical beginnings in
1792, when Richard Murdock in England
first lit his own house by means of gas, and
by the end of the century there were
positive plans to introduce the system to
the States.

To most people, however, the introduction of gas as a lighting medium was a
matter of suspicion concerning its safety,
its economy and even its religious implica-
tions. A German newspaper in 1819
published an article which denounced the
artificial illumination of streets by saying,
'God had decreed that darkness should
follow light, and mortals have no right to
turn night into day.' Other widespread
objections were that gas 'poisoned the air',
that street lighting would 'lower the
standard of morality', or would 'make
robbers bold and cause horses to shy.'

Both Baltimore and Philadelphia had limited gas light as far back as 1807; Baltimore adopted it in 1816, and Boston was converted by 1820. New York was the third city to introduce gas lighting on a large scale, when, in 1823, the New York Gas Light Co., was incorporated with Mr. Samuel Leggett as its first president. His house at No. 7 Cherry Street, was the first residence in New York to be illuminated by gas.

Other installations followed in steady succession, especially after the laying of the first gas mains in Broadway in 1825. On October 23rd, 1826, the New York Theatre (later the Bowery Theatre) was opened as the first theatre to be lit by gas, an enterprise which, in spite of public apprehension concerning the 'light without a wick', attracted as much novelty interest as did the performance itself.

In 1827, the former wooden street lamps, with their oil lanterns, were replaced by cast-iron standards and brightly burning gas jets, which, in the interests of economy, were not required to be lighted on moon-light nights. The Manhatten Gas Light Co. was incorporated in 1830; New Orleans took to gas in 1835, and Cincinnati in 1841.

Many gasoliers and burners were imported from England and France, the French ones being especially decorative, and the English ones being especially efficient. The best features of both sources provided locally manufactured models of good quality and of designs appropriate to the period.

Improvements were also to feature in the new lighting medium, and in 1870 the Mutual Gas Light Co. was the first to manufacture coal gas enriched with naphtha, an addition that produced a gas flame of about twenty candle power.

In the early days, lighting by gas was more costly than the comparable output of oil lamps, and in spite of the risk of fire due to misuse, some fire insurance companies regarded it as being safer than electricity at the time when electric light was in its infancy.

However, gas had several advantages over other illuminants. While kerosene lamps were cheaper than gas installations, there was always the cost of replacement chimneys and wicks to add to the cost of lamp oil, and the time-consuming task of cleaning, trimming and filling. Gas burners were cleaner. The gas itself presented less of a fire risk than oils, and it was ready for instant use at any time.

The one defect of the system was in the fast deterioration of the burners, or in the use of badly made burners, the latter being responsible for poor light, wasted gas, and difficulty in managing the flame.

For optimum results it was necessary to regulate the air supply to the flame by using suitably shaped globes, and, in the case of Argand burners, by the use of glass chimneys. The Sugg 'London' Argand burner, using twenty-four holes and a low-pressure delivery, was, for a time, the best burner available, until the Gleason Manufacturing Company produced the 'noise-less' Argand burner which eliminated the irritating hiss that emitted from other designs.

Other improvements and modifications produced the Siemens Precision burner, the Grand gas lamp, the Niagara Argand, the Royal Argand, the Gordon-Mitchell high powered lamp, and the Morey incandescent burner, to mention but a few of the many patents applied for, and to say nothing of the many that were rejected.

Until about 1878, gas lighting was the only means of lighting the streets and squares, and by 1880 New York City was supplied by no less than nine gas companies, whose directors looked with apprehension at the experiments being carried out to light the streets by means of arc lamps.

The early demonstrations with arc lights powered by electric cells had discouraged confidence in their potential as a general lighting medium, but since about 1870, after the electric generator had been introduced, constant power could be made available. A race to invent and patent designs and systems for arc-lights ensured the fast development of the new light, and for a while the eventual domination of the arc-lamp or the gas-lamp seemed to be in the balance.

The brilliant arc burned with an unpleasant glare and a noisy discharge between its electrodes, factors which precluded its use from most interiors and made it suitable only for railway stations, goods yards and roads. Within a short time after its introduction it was not considered to be a serious opponent, and the gas companies would no doubt have enjoyed many more years of their monopoly had it not been for the inventor Thomas Alva Edison, to whom the gas-lit streets represented only a minor advance in modern illumination techniques, and who saw in the future the possibility of lighting whole cities by means of electricity.

In 1878, he had remarked to a friend, 'I believe the day is coming when all our great waterfalls will become sources of electrical power . . . I believe that a means will be found to utilise them to give us electric light for our homes and factories.'

Almost at once Edison set about the task of inventing the light that was to be the ultimate in domestic and public lighting. He discarded the electric arc as an impractical source of light and recognised the need to control the discharge and to contain it within a glass envelope where it could become incandescent and radiate its luminosity all around.

In his laboratory at Menlo Park, Edison worked on one experiment after another for several months until his decision to use a platinum wire filament inside an evacuated glass bulb brought the most encouraging results so far – a lamp which gave a light intensity of twenty-five candle power as against the five candle power of filaments burning in air.

Whereas his first lamp had lasted for barely eight minutes the new vacuum lamp continued to burn for several minutes longer before the vacuum broke down and the filament melted.

Having established the principle, it remained for him to find a more durable, less expensive filament, and to provide it with a better vacuum in which to work without deterioration.

During the October of 1879, and following many tedious experiments, the inventor made a filament of carbonised thread which he sealed into an evacuated glass bulb. When the current was applied to the conductors this lamp gave a most satisfactory light, and continued its remarkable performance for forty-five hours. Edison's 'bottled sunshine' was capable of turning night into day, without smell, without noise and without the dangers attendant on oil lamps and gas light.

Work with a new kind of filament produced a lamp which burned for two hundred hours, but it was not until he had invented a six hundred hours lamp that he felt ready to demonstrate his achievements to a wider and more influential audience.

He had already received a great deal of acclaim through *The New York Herald,* and many people were following with interest the periodic stories of his experiments.

Edison selected New Year's Eve to open Menlo Park to everyone who wished to attend his demonstration party of lighting by electricity. On the Eve of 1880, thousands of persons from Philadelphia and New York arrived at the station which served Menlo Park, and their impression of the scene that met their eyes was one of the most remarkable in history. The road leading from the station up to the inventor's laboratory was brilliantly lit by hundreds of electric lamps strung between the trees, and as people travelled on foot or by carriage to see the wonders at the other end, a steady snow-shower imparted a fairytale atmosphere to the scene.

The excited visitors saw many marvels of lighting by electricity, including dynamos and generators, and lamps that continued to burn brightly even when immersed in water.

The occasion succeeded in convincing his visitors that there was in fact a future for the electric light. Edison obtained a patent on his incandescent lamp in the January of 1880, the first of nearly 170 to be granted during the next few months.

In his quest for a more efficient filament Edison settled on Japanese bamboo, which,

when suitably processed, was so successful that it was used in millions of bulbs before its eventual relinquishment in favour of an even more successful cellulose mixture.

At the time when Edison opened a new lamp manufactory in Harrison, New Jersey, each lamp was costing him $.25 to make. It took three years of hard work and mechanical improvement to drop this cost to 50c., and a further year to get it down to 22c.; at which point the profits of one year's trading wiped out the deficits of previous years of near-bankruptcy.

At the age of thirty-two, and already famed for his many inventions, Edison arrived in New York ready to set about the task of lighting the great city, but, as one can imagine in 1881, Edison and his staff were among the very few who knew anything at all about lighting by electricity. There was no industry for making electrical components, no more than there were trained electricians to install and maintain them. Everything had to be invented, then made and tested before any forecast could be ventured concerning its safety, its suitability and its probability of success.

Undaunted by the magnitude of the task which he alone could undertake, Edison began to establish the organisation necessary for his purpose – to light one square mile of New York City as the first stage of his unprecedented plan, an initial contract requiring the run of some eighteen miles of cable from south of Wall Street up to Canal Street and from Broadway to the East River.

Special factories had to be established to handle the tremendous tasks of making the equipment and training the men for their roles in the newly-born industry.

From his headquarters at 65 Fifth Avenue, Edison directed the growth of his companies. The old-established Etna Iron Works on Goerck Street on the east side of the city became the Edison Machine Works, which produced the first of the large-scale dynamos.

Meters, switches, sockets and cut-outs were made at a factory in Wooster Street. All the underground equipment such as conductors, piping and junction boxes was made by the Edison Electric Tube Company at 65 Washington Street. The original generator and distribution plant was the Pearl Street Central Station at 257 Pearl Street.

And in the midst of all this activity, Edison still found time to seize every opportunity of demonstrating his expertise with electric light. For example, the sailing ship *Jeannette* was due for an expedition to the North Pole, and under Edison's direction was commissioned completely fitted-out with power supply and electric light. It was a triumphant departure, but during the voyage the vessel ran into heavy ice flows and was destroyed.

Fortunately a further opportunity soon presented itself in the new steamship *Columbia,* into which Edison built a complete lighting system, including generators and deck lights. The sight of that first gaily lighted ship on its seven-week-long maiden voyage must have struck wonder into the hearts of all who saw her, for wherever she docked or anchored, the lights were switched on for all to admire. Sightseers came from miles around to see the floating electric city, and there never had been so much excitement in California since the gold rush.

Edison's enterprise knew no bounds. He organised a parade in which hundreds of men marched down Fifth Avenue wearing helmets fitted with electric lamps, and on another occasion he equipped ballet girls with four hundred lamps and lighted wands.

Meanwhile, the real work of preparing the lighting installation for lower New York continued at the highest possible speed. Workmen dug trenches for the cables, and laid mains at the rate of one thousand feet per day, while trained crews put wiring, sockets, switches and metres into private houses and business premises. By the next summer nine hundred buildings had been fitted out with something like fourteen thousand lamps.

The last piece of major equipment to be built was the giant electric generator for the Pearl Street Power Station. It weighed twenty-eight tons and developed one hundred and fifty horse power at seven hundred revolutions per minute.

The final checks on the equipment and installation were made over Sunday, September 3rd, and during the morning of Monday 4th 1883; and at three o'clock that afternoon, from the offices of Drexel & Morgan, the frock-coated Edison gave word to switch on the lights of New York.

With a sudden blaze of the brightest artificial light ever seen, thousands of lamps throughout the district came to life, astonishing and delighting the occupants of houses, shops and offices in which they were installed. A typically elegant drawing room scene of the early Edison period is depicted in Plate 85 and shows a family at leisure beneath the bright illumination from a centre fitting and two brackets, so

85 *A salon in New York, lit by Edison lamps.*

placed as to shed their light over the piano.

The Edison Electric Illuminating Company of New York was now a formidable opponent of the already powerful gas companies, as the work commenced to build more generators and the power stations to house them.

In all of his concentrated efforts to invent an acceptable system of lighting by electricity, Edison had been in fierce competition with England's Joseph Swan, who, by the December of 1880 had successfully lit his own home, a shop premises, and the mansion of Sir William Armstrong at Cragside near Newcastle.

Whereas, Swan found his success in a lamp filament of squirted cellulose, Edison's forte was his power station and distribution system, the combined principles of which represented an immeasurably important advance in the lighting technology of the period. If months of tedious experiment were to be avoided on both sides of the Atlantic, the time had come for a compromise of co-operation between the two great inventors, and in 1883, Edison went to England, where, as already mentioned, he and Swan joined forces.

Back in the States it seemed certain that Edison's electric light must render the arc light obsolete, and eventually replace gas as the principal lighting medium. Certainly the further development of the arc lamp was arrested, and it is probable that the popularity of gas would have rapidly diminished both abroad and at home had it not been for the introduction of the Welsbach incandescent mantles between 1885 and 93.

These provided a much needed improvement in flame control, and in the brilliance of the light, and were directly responsible for a general resurgence of lighting by gas, especially as it was likely to take a long time to build and install the equipment needed for the new electricity.

The exciting re-birth of gas-lighting lasted right up to the end of the Century, when a further invention – the inverted gas burner – gave another unexpected boost to the industry. For the first time it was possible to design gas fittings with downward turned arms, thus giving the much needed downward spread of light not available from previous designs or open burners. Inverted burners were the latest in modifications in 1905, allowing for a shorter, less fragile mantle, a stronger light and a welcome economy in the use of gas.

In 1908, incandescent mantle burners in candle form were being made by the Enos Company of New York City. There was also a thriving industry in the making of glass shades which were needed to protect the eyes from glare and to conceal the flame from draughts. They were either plainly made or ornamental according to requirements and price, and the best type of shade had to be of certain dimensions and shape, since experience had established that they needed to be mounted at the correct height relative to the burner, or of a certain design to cause good combustion and to burn gas economically.

Globes made of white or opal glass gave a soft mellow light, but these and coloured globes absorbed light and wasted gas by the necessity of increasing the light output to make up for it.

The industry continued to produce hurricane shades for candle holders, outer shades and chimneys for oil lamps, an increased selection of designs for gas lamps, and similar patterns to shade and diffuse the exceptionally bright electric bulbs. With these several alternatives to choose from, the future of lighting seemed to be in the balance, with extremely efficient paraffin lamps and lampadiers in widespread use, the well-tried recently improved gas-light beckoning an even greater consumer population, and the infantile electric light staring defiantly from one new installation after another.

The period between 1900 and 1914 was rich in lighting fittings of all kinds, and those made for lamps, candles, gas and electricity were commonly found in the same household, each serving its individual purpose according to the needs of the family.

Many traditional chandeliers in Colonial and Federal styles remained in constant family service, while others were soon replaced in favour of the new electroliers with their cut glass shades and their unflickering light.

The established taste for traditional designs ensured their continuation in the styles of electroliers, and one in particular is typical of the period. It is composed of a central shaft forming a well-shaped urn,

86 Electrolier.

with rams heads joined by swags of laurel as the principal motif. The lower end of the shaft flares into a shallow milled edge basin with gadrooning on its under side. Six scroll arms, overlaid with leaf tips, radiate around the body, each bearing a cone-shaped lamp cover and a cut-glass shade (Plate 86).

According to individual choice this fitting could be purchased in a variety of finishes, and was currently advertised as being available in gilt, bronze, brass, silver or copper.

Such fittings were common and could be purchased from the many lighting showrooms that now served every principal town and city, while for commercial use, in hotels, public buildings and mansions, they could be made in sizes proportionate to their intended environment, with larger bodies, longer arms and more lights.

It is still of interest to note that in principle there was little change in design from the basic forms of the old chandeliers and lanterns, and that in the silhouette of many a modern fitting of the early Twentieth Century it was possible to detect the unmistakable outline of the old Moorish lamp or Georgian chandelier.

And with this observation we must reluctantly draw our book to a close, for like history itself, this is a story to which an end can never be written. Lighting techniques and lighting fittings are in a state of continuous development, and periods of design are always in the making, so that at sometime in the distant future our particular part of this century will become a period in its own right, and historians will look back through their catalogues and photographs to identify our fashions and furnishing styles.

In their quest to reveal the past, let us hope that they too will find pleasure in the golden days of period lighting.

APPENDIX ONE

THE CHANGING SHAPE OF CANDLE ARMS

1 Thirteenth–Fourteenth Centuries; a spiked sconce driven into a wooden sphere which was suspended on chain or rope.

2 Fourteenth–Fifteenth Centuries; an improved version, with removable branches.

3 Twelfth–early Seventeenth Centuries; a remarkable record of popularity and functional service. Modifications to design separate the periods during which these fittings were made.

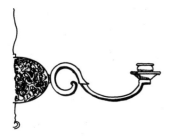

4 Haddon Hall design, c.1660, a skilful deviation from the Dutch style.

5 Knole House design c.1670; a complete break from previous baluster and ball design.

6 Queen Anne period c.1710; with knopped arms and an overlay of leafwork.

7 Georgian 'door knocker' arm; c.1820 or earlier.

8 Rococo period, c.1760.

9 Louis XVI, Hunting Horn applique, c.1774.

10 Empire design, c.1810; showing the cornucopia-shaped arm.

11 Regency, Griffin bracket, c.1812.

THE CHANGING SHAPE OF CANDLESTICKS

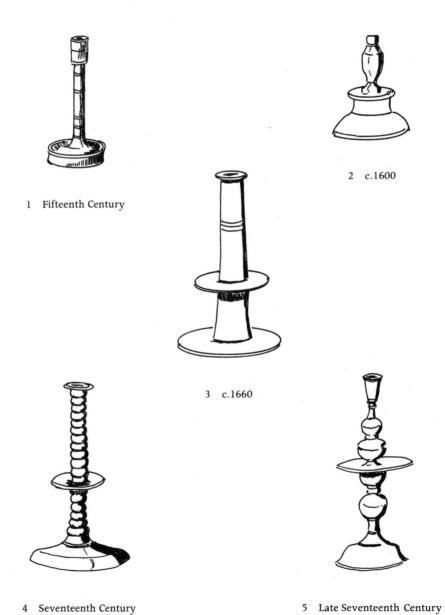

1   Fifteenth Century

2   c.1600

3   c.1660

4   Seventeenth Century

5   Late Seventeenth Century

6   c.1718

8   c.1775

7   c.1759

9   c.1820

10   c.1900

THE CHANGING SHAPE OF OIL LAMPS

1   Roman hand lamp First Century

2   Crusie Sixteenth/Seventeenth Century

3   Glass Float lamp

4   Cardan's lamp 1550

5   Miles's 'agitable' lamp c.1787

6   Argand's lamp c.1784

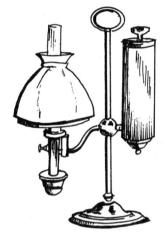

8   Student lamp c.1830

7   Rumford's lamp c.1800

9   Hitchcock's lamp 1880

10   Paraffin lamp, late Nineteenth Century

THE CHANGING SHAPE OF GAS LAMPS

1 Duplex Fishtail burner
   1820–30

2 Union jet 1820–30

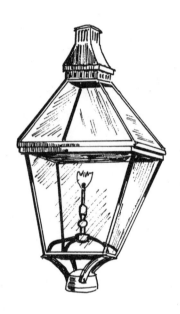

5 Street lamp. Mid-
   Nineteenth Century

3 Batswing burner 1820–30.
   Introduced 1816.

4 Ratstail burner 1820–30.
   Earliest type before 1808.

6 Table lamp with Argand-
type multi-burner. 1874

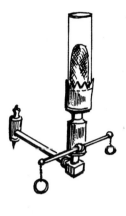

7 Bracket burner with
mantle c.1890

8 Gas table lamp c.1895

9 Gasolier c.1900

10 Inverted burner with
mantle c.1903.

APPENDIX TWO

THE ART OF MATCHING FITTINGS WITH FURNITURE

1   Gothic

2   Early Tudor

3   Elizabethan

4   Stuart

5   Commonwealth

6   Carolean

7   William & Mary

8   Queen Anne

9   William Kent

10   Louis XV

11   Chippendale

12   Louis XVI

13   Robert Adam

14   Hepplewhite

15   Empire

16   Victorian

INDEX

Page numbers in *italic* indicate an illustration.

Adam, Robert, 99
Argand, Aimé, 54, 103, 108
Argand Lamp, 63, 103, *108*, 109, 138–9, 146

Barroco, The, 72, *73*
Betty Lamp, 131–2
Boulle, Charles Andre, 42
Boulton, Matthew, 99
Braccio, 26
Braccio Cresset, *24*
Brighton Royal Pavilion, 109–11

Candelabra, 40, 94
Candélabre, 59, 60, 61
Candelabro, 25, *26*, 67, 70, 73
Candelier, 26, *31*, 40
Candeliero, 32
Candlesticks, 22, 38, 68, 80, 90, 93, 97, *98*, 99, *100*, 101, *132*, *137*
Candil 35
Cardan's Lamp, 39–40, 50
Chandelier, 35–7, *38*, 40, 41, 54, 55, *83*, 84, *85*, *86*, 87, 90–3, *95*, *97*, *102*, 106, 111, 123, 133, *141*
Christian's Lamps, 19
Colbert, Jean Baptiste, 43
Colonial Period, 130
Colza Oil, 55
Corona, 25, 35, 47, 69, *73*
Cresset, 24
Crusie, 48

Davy, Sir Humphrey, 123–4

Dinanderie Candlesticks, 82
Directoire, 56
Directoire Applique, *57*
Drummond, Capt. Thomas, 123
Du Barry, The Countess, 50

Edwardian Period, 127
Edison, Thomas Alva, 147–50
Electrolier, *127*, 128, 152
Empire Period, 59

Falconet, 58
Farole, 67
Federal Period, 136
Final, 67, *71*
Flambeau, 36, 40, 58

Gasoliers, 110, *111*
Gas Table Lamps, *121*
Georgian Lanterns, 113–4
Georgian Period, 96
Gibbons, Grinling, 89
Glass Lamps, 84
Glass Peg Lamps, *51*
Godet, 36
Gótico Period, 68

Hand Lamp, 19, 78–9
Hanging Lamp, *20*
Hitchcock Lamp, 143–4
Hope, Thomas, 105

Iron Gothic Lantern, *23*

Kent, William, 97

Lamerie, Paul de, 97
Lampada, *28*, 67
Lampadaire, *63*, 115
Lampadario, 27
Lampara, 66, *74*
Lampier, 36
Lampione, 26, 29
Lucerna, 24, *32*, 64
Lumière, *30*

Marine Lamp, *117*
Mariposa, 76
Moderatore Lamp, 64
Moorish Period, 67–8
Mosque Lamp, 77
Murdock, Richard, 104

Palmatoria, 66, 76
Pan Lamp, 35
Paraffin Lamp, *118*, 119
Parker, William, 100
Patent Lamp, 138
Pompadour, The Marquise de, 50

Régence Period, 44, *45*
Regency Period, 105
Renaissance-Tudor Period, 82
Ribbon-Bow Applique, *53*
Rocaille, 45
Rococo, 45, *46*
Romanico Period, 68
Rush Holder, 130, *131*

Sconce, *83*, *89*, *93*
Specchi Colle Lumiere, 29
Stone Lamp, *40*
Stuart Period, 87
Student Lamp, *64*, 112
Sugg Burner, 120–1
Swan, Joseph, 124, *125*

Torciere, 25

Velon, 66
Victorian Period,

Watteau, Antoine, 43
Wick Spout Lamp, 35
Winsor, Frederick Albert, 104